A Season on the Allegheny

Robert T. Hilliard

Copyright © 2012 Robert T. Hilliard

All rights reserved. No part of this book may be reproduced, stored, or transmitted without the prior written consent of the author.

ISBN-10: 1475201168
ISBN-13: 978-1475201161

For my beautiful, loving wife Pamela. Thank you for encouraging, contributing, enabling, tolerating, and, most importantly, believing.

and

In fond memory of Hunter, the best gray-haired hunting partner I could ever hope to have.

CONTENTS

	Preface	i
	Allegheny National Forest Map	
1	By the Numbers	1
2	Buzzard's Luck	13
3	Thrill Ride	23
4	The Thousandth Acre Deer	47
5	Pheasants on the Forest	67
6	The Forest for the Trees	79
7	Talking Turkey	99
	Photos	115
8	Of Bears and Boys	131
9	Traditions	157
10	Wilderness on the Water	197
11	Snowshoeing	221
12	Regeneration	237
13	Howling Wilderness	253
14	Shades of Gray	285
15	Spring Ahead, Look Back	299
	End Notes	315

Preface

In the spring of 2004, I was lying awake in bed pondering topics for upcoming magazine articles. As usual, my thought process was geared not only toward making a dollar, but how I could best enjoy the time spent afield while that dollar was being made. Since much of my outdoor writing has been geared toward public land destinations, my train of thought was traveling along that track.

As I sifted through a mental list of hunting destinations that I hadn't yet covered in my home state of Pennsylvania, it occurred to me that I had somehow managed to bypass one of my favorite places: the Allegheny National Forest. I quickly began to inventory destinations and issues within the Forest that I thought might impress a magazine editor sufficiently to bankroll my hunting trip.

The list grew long rather quickly: Wild and Scenic Rivers, virgin forest, deer management, lawsuits over timber cutting. Man, I thought as I stared into the ceiling fan, you could write a whole book about all the stuff that's going on in the Allegheny National Forest. Hey, wait a minute…

I considered waking my wife Pam to share the idea with her at that very moment. But, discretion being the better part of marriage, I decided to wait till morning.

Luckily, when the next morning rolled around, Pam greeted my brainstorm with enthusiasm rather than ridicule. Since she has been my brainstorm litmus test for the better part of my adult life, I considered that a great sign.

The book that resulted from that moment of inspiration is a chronicle of the events of one year of hunting within the boundaries of the Allegheny National Forest ("on the Forest" as the US Forest Service staffers like to say). Beginning with the resident goose season in September and ending with the spring gobbler season in May, I hunted nearly every available season and recorded the people, places, and perspectives that I encountered within the Half-Million-Acre Woods.

Although this book is intended to highlight the multitude of hunting opportunities on the Allegheny, it also travels well beyond the bounds of standard hunting destination fare. Rather than revealing the location of the absolute best grouse cover on the Allegheny (as if I would) or which patch of brush that 10-point buck is hiding behind (as if I knew), these pages focus at least as much on the issues swirling around the Forest: its natural history, its industrialized past, and its controversial present.

As might be expected, there were a huge number of people who were critical to the telling of this story and I'd suffer endless guilt if I didn't take a shot at thanking at least some of them. First on the list, of course, is Pam, who tolerated the weekly absences and the soaring gasoline costs with amazing fortitude. For her indulgence – as well as that of our kids, Rachel, Stephanie, and Jacob – I will be forever grateful.

Then there were the folks that helped me keep the project going. I called upon Ric Harris, my friend and sounding board, too many times. When I asked him to make some sense of the mess I had tangled together, he helped me work through the knots every time. I might have somehow gotten through it without his advice (not to mention his excellent work on the cover layout) but it would have certainly been a different – and lesser quality – book.

Like Scarlet O'Hara in brush pants and orange cap, I frequently relied on the kindness of others. Amazingly, not one of them tossed me out on my backside. Ken Stockert and Dan Brophy both pitched in with lodging and guide services on multiple occasions; folks like Mark Banker, John Mack, Scott Blum, and Nate Welker let me enjoy the considerable talents of their canine hunting companions; and my indomitable duck-hunting partner, Dan Fitzgerald, just keeps coming back for more. I am indebted to all of them for indulging me.

No list of acknowledgements would be complete without thanking the capable and remarkably helpful staff that the US Forest Service has assembled on the Allegheny. Brad Nelson, Pam Thurston, Rick Kandare, and Mark Conn were among those that jumped to my aid in providing the needed background material. They have my endless appreciation.

The one USFS staffer to whom I am obliged above all is the dedicated and diligent Mary Hosmer. Despite their volume and frequency, Mary continually filled my pain-in-the-rump information requests with answers that were both timely and thorough. She constantly impressed me with her understanding of issues related to the Allegheny National Forest and with her personal commitment to conservation causes. And on top of all that, she invited me to go snowshoe hare hunting with her. She is a true professional and meeting her was one of the highlights of the entire project.

Through the generous contributions of the folks listed above and dozens more that I've accidentally overlooked, I was able to enjoy some of the greatest adventures of my life and to share them on these pages. From Wilderness Areas to white-tailed deer, from ghost towns to grouse dogs, there are countless threads that make up the rich tapestry of the Allegheny National Forest. The following chapters will introduce just a few of those threads. I only hope that I've conveyed them in a way that allows others to experience even a part of the pleasure and wonder that I discovered during my season on the Allegheny.

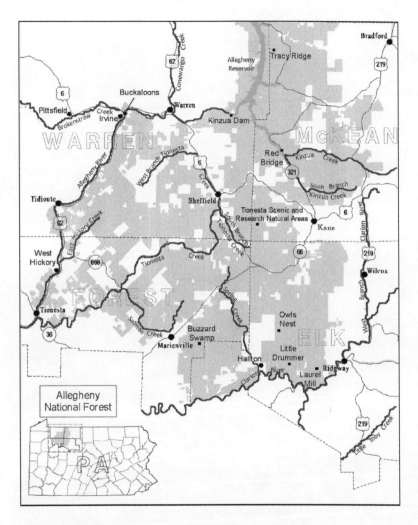

Allegheny National Forest Map

Courtesy of Thomas Rockwell

CHAPTER 1
BY THE NUMBERS

They belong to you and me. The National Forests – all 191 million acres of them – exist for the hunter and the hiker, the forester and the family, the timber cutter and the tree hugger. They're ours. Remember that.

Truthfully, I wish I had realized that sooner. As a kid, each family visit to the Allegheny National Forest (located just a three-hour drive from our western Pennsylvania home) seemed like a journey to a far-off wonderland full of massive trees, craggy cliffs, and boulder-strewn creeks. Always announced by the phrase "We're going up to the mountains," these fall foliage trips were as much a part of our autumn ritual as jack-o-lanterns and stuffed turkeys.

As I marveled at the sights out the back window of our wood-paneled station wagon, the official signs proclaiming

"National Forest Boundary" and "Allegheny National Forest – Land of Many Uses" seemed to declare that this ground was different, set apart from the rest. Thus my first perception of National Forests was that they were like a glass-encased museum exhibit, something to be touched only gently, if at all. It never occurred to me that a National Forest might be a playground, full of the most gorgeous and rugged toys that nature could devise. And it certainly never occurred that I, the eight-year-old in the Terry Bradshaw jersey and striped tube socks, might own it.

Our Allegheny National Forest covers 513,000 acres in northwestern Pennsylvania, butting against the New York border. Draped across Elk, Forest, McKean, and Warren counties, the Allegheny has been ours since 1923, the year that President Calvin Coolidge gave the OK to create it.

Although its rolling mountains are tame by western standards, the Allegheny's glacier-rounded peaks – as high as 2,263 feet and incised throughout by sparkling streams – are a key ingredient in its allure. However, the one defining feature of the Allegheny, the element that draws nearly a million and a half visitors each year, is the forest itself. Virtually every square mile on the Allegheny today is blanketed by the tough generation of trees that sprung forth after the forest's systematic annihilation a century ago.

Before the first documented European exploration of this region in 1749, the woods within the area that is now the Allegheny National Forest were dominated by centuries-old beech and hemlock trees that towered over more than 60 percent of the forest floor.[1] Immediately, though, those trees began to fall to the axes of the first pioneers. The first sawmill was established in Warren County barely 50 years after the first documented exploration of the region and by 1801 about 30,000 feet of white pine timbers from this mill, lashed together to create huge timber rafts, were floated down the Allegheny River to Pittsburgh.[2]

The region's white pine was prized by the boat-building industry for its buoyancy and strength, but the land that later formed the National Forest also produced everything from clothes pins to Louisville Sluggers. It was discovered that the trees could be used to make charcoal, acetic acid, and, most importantly, hemlock tannin. The latter product made the region's hemlocks – considered a trash species by earlier loggers – a precious commodity and established northern Pennsylvania as the center of the world's leather tanning industry.

Beginning in the 1880s, the advent of railroads to haul out felled trees accelerated the devastation of the forests and by the early twentieth century, timber barons had cut nearly every valuable stick and wrung every available cent from the once lush land. And then they simply left, moving their operations to literally greener territory in the American West. When the barren and fire-ravaged terrain they left behind was added to the National Forest system, cynics called it the "Allegheny Brushland" and the "Great Pennsylvania Desert."

Slowly, though, as fire control techniques advanced and the US Forest Service's concept of forestry management took shape, the astounding power of nature asserted itself and the Allegheny actually started to earn the title of National Forest. When the new forest materialized in the years surrounding World War II, my personal connection to the Allegheny was also sown, albeit decades before my birth. It was then that both my grandfather and great-grandfather bought camps just a few miles from the National Forest boundary.

Though they both sold their shares in the camps long before my existence was even considered, my parents never failed to point out the locations during our trips to the mountains. I can still recall my wonder at the fact that our family, my very own Granddad Kenny and Pappap Shook, once held a piece of this special land for themselves.

I also clearly remember my amazement at the miniscule garage next to Pappap's camp. When I speculated aloud as to what kind of tiny car he must have parked in there, my folks had to struggle through their peals of laughter to explain the workings of an outhouse.

My warmest childhood memory of the Allegheny was an afternoon spent at Camp Shanley, the property in which Granddad Kenny had once owned a stake. Many of the details are now blurred, but vestiges of the emotions that swirled within my pre-teen chest that day still remain. There was the pounding anticipation as I slid my plastic rifle into the trunk next to Dad's .32-caliber Marlin, wrapped in its soft leather case; my exuberance at being included with the men as they shot targets instead of being coddled with the wives and younger kids back at camp; and a confusing mix of pride and sheepishness when I was allowed a small sip of blackberry brandy, served in teacups as we sat rocking on the camp's high front porch that evening.

It was heady stuff, my first halting steps toward adulthood. The three decades since have dulled my recollection of the names and faces from that day, but I still sometimes think of the view from that porch as the sun disappeared over the ridge.

And the trees. The forest I stood in that day, and so many days since, helped fuel my desire to study nature. And that burning curiosity about the natural world eventually led to my career as an environmental biologist. In a sense, those awe-inspiring, cloud-scraping, stretching-for-miles trees have become a part of me. And I still long to be a part of them.

The trees on the Allegheny today, the resilient forest that emerged from the onslaught of the Industrial Revolution, is distinctly different from the previous forest, irrevocably altered by timbering, fire (and today, fire suppression), white-tailed deer browsing, acid rain, and innumerable other factors. Red maple and black cherry now comprise about half of the Allegheny's woods, with the previously-dominant hemlock and beech reduced nearly to afterthoughts.

True to its roots, the Allegheny still leads all other National Forests in USFS Region 9 (Eastern Region) in timber production, due mostly to the value of its world famous black cherry timber. In the twenty-first century, however, logging is planned on a "sustainable yield" basis, ensuring that our forest resources will still be there when we need them. Guided by their *Land and Resource Management Plan*, or "Forest Plan," the USFS today considers ecological factors, timber needs, recreation impacts, and public input before determining how forest resources will be allotted.

While protecting the last shards of virgin forest and critical recreation sites from the chainsaw, this multiple use concept still allows resource extraction to occur, albeit markedly below historic levels. For example, while the current harvest for all tree species on the Allegheny is about 6,300 acres a year, each one of the dozens of tanneries that dotted the region in the 1890s would have gnawed through about 5,000 acres of hemlock annually – and hemlock was only one component of that era's logging industry.[3]

To keep up with changing demands upon forest resources, the USFS prefers to update Forest Plans every 10 to 15 years under normal circumstances. But then circumstances on the Allegheny have been far from normal since the last plan was implemented in 1986. The delay started with two years of Forest Service planning process review in Congress, and was lengthened by lawsuits against the Allegheny National Forest over its timber cutting policies. Sprinkle in some personnel changes at the local level and this National Forest ends up operating in 2005 under a plan that was put in place the same year that "We Are the World" topped the music charts.

This isn't to suggest that the Allegheny's Forest Plan hasn't changed at all in the last two decades. On the contrary, it has been amended 11 times, ranging from the mundane, such as changes addressing new developments in herbicide technology, to the magnificent, like the addition of both the Allegheny and Clarion Rivers to the National Wild and Scenic Rivers Program.

The federal Wild and Scenic designation acknowledges that these two largest waterways on the Forest are the fulcrum of a spectacular network of over 700 miles of streams, some of which offer fishing opportunities that rival any in the country. In fact, the Pennsylvania state record northern pike and walleye were both taken from the Allegheny Reservoir, the 12,000-acre impoundment of the Allegheny River in the northeastern corner of the Forest. Though it's not the only impoundment on the Forest, the Allegheny Reservoir's combination of fishing, boating, swimming, water skiing, boat-in camping, and hunting make it the centerpiece of the National Forest's water-based recreation.

When it comes to recreation, however, aquatic activities are only part of the action. According to a recent visitor survey, most people come to the Allegheny just to "hang out," and there is no shortage of places to do just that. For starters, there's the 23,100-acre Allegheny National Recreation Area, the 8,570-acre Hickory Creek Wilderness, the 362-acre Allegheny Islands Wilderness, the 2,018-acre Tionesta National Scenic Area, and the 122-acre Hearts Content National Scenic Area, all of which offer fantastic spots to hang out for a few hours, or even days. And if you're looking to push harder than that, there are over 200 miles of designated hiking trails on the Allegheny, ranging from short, flat, handicapped-accessible trails to 86 long and rugged miles of the North Country National Scenic Trail.

Maybe the thought of sitting pensively among the white pines at Hearts Content or backpacking the North Country Trail doesn't get it done for you. Perhaps you prefer your trail experience with a little more adrenaline and a lot more horsepower. If that's the case, the Allegheny's got your fix there too, with over 100 miles of designated off-road trails for ATVs and motorcycles, and 366 miles of snowmobile routes when the white stuff flies.

And then, of course, there is the hunting. Historically, a "wide variety of wildlife inhabited the forests of the Allegheny Plateau prior to white settlement. Of the larger animals, deer, elk, bear, wolves, cougars, wildcats, and lynx were all present."[4] At that time, the Indians of the Iroquois Confederacy (aka the Five Nations, made up of the Seneca, Onondaga, Tuscarora, Oneida, and Mohawk tribes) hunted extensively in the area that is now the Allegheny National Forest. For decades after, the early white settlers continued to enjoy the bounty that the mountains had to offer.

Until the Pennsylvania Game Commission (PGC) was formed in 1895, few game laws existed and there were virtually no restrictions on seasons or bag limits. With an ever-increasing number of settlers taking what they needed from the land, professional hunters plying their trade, and millions of acres of forest being cleared down to the last twig, animals quickly began to disappear from the Pennsylvania landscape.

Due to bounties placed by the state, wolves were among the first to vanish. One report states that the last bounty collected in Pennsylvania was on a wolf killed in Warren

County in 1866.⁵ The Eastern elk, a species that once ranged across the entire Keystone State, were eliminated from the most of the commonwealth by the 1840s and a decade later the entire herd was confined to the area in and around what is now the Allegheny National Forest.⁶ Conflicting tales exist, but one of the most commonly told is that the last native elk in Pennsylvania was killed by a Seneca Indian named Jim Jacobs in 1867.

One species that clung to the last few fragments of habitat long enough for help to arrive was the white-tailed deer. By the time the PGC first began to enforce deer harvest laws in 1896, the perilously low deer population was threatening to vanish like the wolves and elk before them. Again, the wild and remote Allegheny region was one of the few locations in which native herds desperately hung on.

Good fortune finally found those tenacious Allegheny National Forest whitetails in the first half of the twentieth century in the form of a rebounding forest resource that provided an abundant supply of forage. As a result, deer populations on the Allegheny rocketed upward. Ironically, less than three decades after taking drastic measures to restore whitetail populations, the PGC had to institute special antlerless seasons within the Forest due to deer damage.

A PGC report from that era gives a fascinating look at both the ascendance of the whitetail population and the growing significance of the Forest as a deer hunting destination. It begins by noting that hunting on the Allegheny National Forest "is very popular with deer hunters far and wide." ⁷ In six different areas within Forest County, the opening day of antlerless season found over 2,000 cars jammed into just 30 miles of road – a hunter's car every 79 feet.

The report goes on to state that "[a] very heavy concentration of deer has existed during the past decade," and that "the 'deer [browse] line' is evident everywhere except in the most recently cutover areas." The Depression Era report then closes with a statement that could just as easily have been last week: "The present day popularity of deer hunting makes it inevitable that more hunters will be disappointed than are successful. The size of the deer herd, however, must be kept in balance with the amount of food available to support it, even though the desire of every hunter to get a deer cannot be satisfied."

Another study from that period lends insight into not only the whitetail population, but also other game species on the relatively new Allegheny National Forest. In the summer and winter of 1935 and the spring of 1936, members of the Civilian Conservation Corps were called upon to develop a game census for the entire Forest by driving (that is, walking side by side through the woods like hunters on a deer drive) designated areas of habitat.

The results of the game drive report are intriguing. This rebounding forest was producing a staggering abundance of game: more than 48,000 deer, 18,000 cottontail rabbits, 9,200 snowshoe hares, 26,000 squirrels, and 37,500 grouse. Equally notable is a game species that was entirely absent from the survey, the wild turkey. Though none were found during the 1935 and 1936 surveys, turkeys are today one of the most abundant game animals on the Allegheny National Forest.

How do these conditions on the adolescent National Forest compare to what exists on the Allegheny today? That, of course, is the question I set out to answer. It led me to search for whitetail tracks in the shade of last remaining giant hemlocks and to chase grouse while shouldering through the stinging brush of a regenerating clearcut. Beyond that, it revealed the history of a region that has been inhabited for over 10,000 years and reminded me of a conservation ethic that dates back more than a century.

More than anything, though, this season on the Allegheny was inspiring. Whether it was a quiet sunrise over a splashing stream or a mountain view more spectacular than I could imagine, each day in the Forest stirred my soul.

And the best part was that I could visit anytime I wanted. After all, the National Forests are ours. Remember that.

CHAPTER 2

BUZZARD'S LUCK

The place names on the Allegheny National Forest fascinate me. They run from the geographical (Klondike, Reno Run, Sheffield) to the meteorological (Thundershower Run, Windy Hill, Lightning Run) to the simply inexplicable (Fools Knob, Jo Jo, Pigs Ear). Others, like Bully Hollow and Lamentation Run, can be at once both melancholy and lyrical.

Buzzard Swamp is none of the above.

This wildlife management area, a mosaic of wetland and upland spreading over about 9,000 acres, is stuck with a handle that, let's face it, not even a momma buzzard could love. Even the streams that flow through Buzzard Swamp, Muddy Fork and Crooked Run, have labels that are uninspiring, to say the least.

But despite its bad luck in the naming department, Buzzard Swamp has been a focal point of conservation efforts for more than four decades. The site's wetlands, in particular, have been created or massaged in some way for the purpose of wildlife habitat improvement since the first cooperative agreement between the USFS and the PGC around 1962.

At that time, Buzzard Swamp was just like much of the rest of the National Forest – a large chunk of cut-over land with sparse patches of briars and saplings struggling to survive. But someone within the PGC apparently recognized that this particular piece of ground, with its high water table and flat, open topography, could be transformed into a unique resource for waterfowl. Once work started in earnest, bulldozers gouged out more than 300 pothole wetlands within two years. At the same time, the PGC was constructing dams to create larger open water habitats at Buzzard Swamp. The biggest of these is 66-acre Impoundment #6 (talk about your unattractive names), but the most important is #6's upstream neighbor, the pond that forms the main attraction of the 40-acre wildlife propagation area.

The propagation area is the Playboy Mansion of Buzzard Swamp: dedicated to sexual activity and off-limits to the general public. Through contributions from the National Wild Turkey Federation, Ducks Unlimited, and other non-profits, it's developed into a sheltered mix of open water, marshy wetlands, and grassy uplands that attracts waterfowl from all over northern Pennsylvania. This breeding area, posted against human trespass and situated in the middle of wetland habitat unlike any other in the region makes Buzzard Swamp one of the best waterfowling destinations in northern Pennsylvania.

And so, when the calendar flipped over to September and the start of our state's resident goose season, my new F-150 pickup was packed and pointed north, with Buzzard Swamp as its destination. The decision to go to the Allegheny that weekend was a last minute one; just the day before our plans for Labor Day weekend had changed and I was suddenly free on Saturday.

Although I felt like I was fairly vibrating with the excitement and promise of a new hunting season, I was practically comatose in comparison to my Weimaraner, Hunter. He careened around the yard like a ball on a roulette wheel as I loaded the truck.

It was the Friday before Labor Day and highway traffic was heavy as I made my way toward the Forest. It seemed every third vehicle I passed on I-80 was a truck loaded with an ATV and firewood. When I passed the sign announcing "Allegheny National Forest This Exit" and half a dozen sets of turn signals came to life in front of me, I knew that a high percentage of this four-wheeler and four-wheel drive crowd was bound for a weekend on the Allegheny.

I suppose that I am like most hunters in that I rarely pay attention to what's happening amid the little hamlets and houses that I pass en route to my hunting destination. Instead I use that time constructively by daydreaming about massive flocks of game birds or staring intently at every field in hopes of finding a deer or turkey standing there. However, since this project is as much about the people and places that surround the Allegheny as the game within it, I turned my eyes away from the meadows and woods and concentrated instead on the lawns and sidewalks.

What I saw was simply people living their lives.

I passed a gauntlet of pastel-clad well-wishers showering newlyweds with rice in front of a tiny white church, and just down the road an attractive woman in a tank top steered a riding mower around her lawn. It suddenly dawned on me that the Allegheny National Forest isn't a concept at all for these folks. It's merely one part of the place they live, perhaps no more or less a part than the school playground, the bowling alley, or the Uni-Mart.

I had hardly begun to ponder this when the last of the permanent residences along my route were swallowed by the woods, leaving only the occasional hunting camp and a bumper crop of tents every few hundred yards along the Clarion River. As I turned onto successively narrower and rougher roads, Hunter became more rambunctious in the back seat, sensing, by some mysterious technique that he's developed over the years, that we were nearing our destination.

Pulling into the pitch black parking lot at Buzzard Swamp, I gulped down a cold sandwich and a bag of chips then proceeded to set up camp. With my eyes now adjusted to the dark and my sensibilities adapting once again to the wilds, it felt wrong to flip on an electric flashlight. I wasn't going to bother with a fire this late in the evening, so I opted to set up the tent with only the light from my oil lantern.

With a stunningly clear night sky above us, I decided to take the gray dog for a quick stroll down one of the maintained trails. We didn't go very far, but as Hunter and I strolled back toward the truck, our footsteps were accompanied by coyote song pealing through the woods. I felt the tickle of raised hair on my neck and shivered involuntarily.

With an early wake-up call ahead, Hunter and I crawled inside the tent and settled for the night. He coiled himself comfortably on top of a corner of my sleeping bag and was soon snoring peacefully while I finished the day with a journal entry. Setting my watch alarm for 4:30 AM, I dialed out the lantern and fell asleep within seconds.

The beeping alarm was an unpleasant start to the morning, but a couple of chocolate doughnuts and a few swigs of Mountain Dew quickly changed my outlook. I gathered my gear and started down the path to Impoundment #6. On an earlier trip I had scoped out a natural blind just a few hundred feet downstream from the dam that forms the propagation area, figuring to intercept geese on their way into that safe haven.

Because the trip to Buzzard Swamp was an eleventh-hour decision, none of my usual hunting partners were available to join me. While that afforded a little more solitude, it also meant I would be gunning with a major handicap – no decoys.

Since I'm only an occasional waterfowler, I've never made an investment in decoys. As it's worked out I've never needed to. Usually I swap the use of my buddies' dekes for upland bird hunting time over Hunter, a trade that all of them are happy to make. But today we would have to do without.

I moved carefully down the trail under the half moon that shone from a startlingly clear pre-dawn sky. Hunter also seemed cautious, never venturing more than a few yards ahead. The natural blind I had selected beforehand was a point where a tall warm season grass patch – planted for waterfowl breeding habitat – changed over to a thinner mix of sedges and woody brush. When I reached the exact spot, though, I got an unpleasant surprise.

There in the glare of my flashlight was the shining hull of an aluminum canoe. Since there was also a decoy bag and assorted other waterfowling paraphernalia stashed nearby, it was quickly apparent that other hunters had already tabbed this blind as their own. Disappointed, I moved further down the shore.

Without a back-up plan, I was now stuck. I stumbled along the uneven bank in the dark, searching for a spot with vegetation tall and thick enough to hide both a 6'2" hunter and an 85-pound Hunter. After a half-dozen spots proved unsuitable, my mood was inching toward furious when I finally found a small knoll overlooking the bank. Luckily, the little rise was covered with a mix of sedges and wool grass just thick enough to shield us from the view of incoming geese.

About 10 minutes after first sunrays crept over my right shoulder, the canoe owners arrived and set up a decoy spread. I was concerned that they would scare off any first light birds, but that worry evaporated when 15, then 30, then

45 minutes went by with no sign of geese anywhere in the white-blue atmosphere.

And then, as if on a fixed schedule, the first flight of geese arrived exactly at 7:30 AM. As they winged their way in from the north, both the canoe gang and I began to hammer away at our calls. When the geese finally became more than specks above the horizon, I tried hard to will them in my direction, envisioning a scenario in which they swung to the east and passed directly in front of me.

That scenario, unfortunately, wasn't one the geese were considering. Disregarding my blasts on the old Sears call, as well as the calls and decoys of the canoe hunters, the birds never veered from a direct line to their intended destination – the safe harbor of the propagation area.

If there was any doubt that this first route was a coincidence, it was quickly erased by the second and third flights of the morning. They also chose an unswerving approach to the propagation area instead of the potential dangers of Impoundment #6.

I deduced that this trend was going to continue. A few straggling singles and doubles convinced me to hang around until late morning, but by then even some sporadic shooting from other ponds to the north had tailed off. I hated to admit it since I hadn't even raised my gun to my shoulder, but it was time to head out.

Taking the scenic route back, Hunter and I rounded the lower end of Impoundment #6. On the other side, I was immediately drawn to a golden field of chest-high warm season grass. Although pheasant season was still almost two months away, I couldn't resist a little training run for the gray dog and he rewarded me by finding two birds, both hens.

Back on the trail, I discovered a vantage point to look down into the propagation area. Through the zoom lens of my camera, I could see five dozen geese paddling around and feeding, safe as the gold in Fort Knox. I decided it was time to move on.

Just a few yards up the trail, Hunter stiffened as he peeked ahead around a bend. He was 30 yards ahead of me, and his upright posture and bristling back hair made me think that another dog was approaching. As I came up behind him, he bolted and disappeared around the curve.

I hustled ahead just in time to see a black form disappear into the brush ahead of Hunter. It took several moments to realize this was not a black Labrador retriever, but a decent sized bear ambling off into the swamp. Thankful that the bruin had run for cover instead of toward my dog, I whistled Hunter back to my side and moved a little more quickly toward the truck.

When we reached the parking area, the non-hunters (sane people who *don't* rise at 4:30 AM) were just getting ready to head into Buzzard Swamp for the day. A middle-aged couple equipped with float tubes and bass rigs stopped for a brief chat at the head of the trail, while a young couple with a brood of preteen kids geared up for a bike ride. The requisite visit between the kids and Hunter – who despises attention with roughly the same spirit that he despises a good sirloin – took up a good fifteen minutes of their riding time, but they didn't seem to mind.

As the young family pedaled off, Hunter and I were alone again. I packed the truck, made a few notes, and sat on the tailgate of the F-150 for a couple minutes more to polish off the leftover doughnuts and Mountain Dew.

After momentarily enjoying the quiet, I picked up a low sound on the light breeze. It took a few seconds, but I soon identified it as the honking of geese drifting up from the propagation area. I couldn't understand them, but I could clearly sense the derision in their tone. I had started this trip mocking the depressing label given to Buzzard Swamp, but now the Swamp, or at least its resident goose population, was mocking my depressing ineptitude as a goose hunter.

It was a fitting end to the day, but I hoped it wasn't a sign of things to come. The last thing I needed at this point was a run of buzzard's luck.

CHAPTER 3

THRILL RIDE

Though the hard luck of the goose hunt gnawed at me, my attention was soon diverted by my next Allegheny adventure: a duck hunting float trip down the Clarion River. I asked Dan Fitzgerald, a soft-spoken, sly-witted railroad engineer, as my partner on this trip.

Dan and I met as flag football teammates, on a squad appropriately known as the Brewzers. While we didn't win many games, we were one of the perennial league leaders in post-game beer consumption. It was during one of these parking lot gatherings, throughout which we alternated the application of ice to our sore limbs with the application of lager to our innards, that Dan and I hatched the idea to go duck hunting. Despite the fact that neither of us had ever tried it before, it seemed like a magnificent idea. In retrospect, it's difficult to assess whether the perceived excellence was due to the beer we were drinking or the multiple blows to the head we received while playing.

I'll spare you the gory details of that first duck hunting trip, except to say that it resulted in me nearly sinking to the bottom of a swollen river then nearly freezing to death once I crawled out. That was just before we missed the only two ducks we shot at. Other than that, it was great.

Incredibly, Dan agreed to a return engagement when I pitched my idea of a float hunt down the Clarion. He was clearly a sucker for duck hunting adventure. Or maybe he was just a sucker.

The 52-mile stretch of the Clarion along the southern boundary of the Allegheny National Forest was designated as a National Wild and Scenic River in 1996, putting it in the company of the Allegheny River as the only two Wild and Scenic waterways on the Allegheny National Forest. Unlike the Allegheny River designation, which was greeted by shrieks of protest, petitions, and the threat of lawsuits, the acceptance of the Clarion was relatively quiet. Perhaps this is because the Clarion River valley, once one of the most active industrial centers in the world, is now largely uninhabited. That is, unless you believe in ghosts.

The Clarion's rough-and-tumble manufacturing years of a century or more ago were documented in a 2003 book entitled *Elk County: A Journey through Time*. It was written by local historian John Imhof, who claims that the valley currently houses more ghost towns than active communities. As Imhof notes in the preface to his book:

"Logging, sawmills, rafting, leather tanning, wood chemical plants and dozens of other wood industries were once found in great numbers in virtually every corner of the county.

"Today, all that has changed. While logging continues to be an important industry in the county, never again will the waters of the Clarion River...carry great loads of lumber to market. No more will the remote hollows hear the mournful call of a steam whistle or the rhythmic whoosh of a crosscut saw. Where great sawmills once stood, only fields and the occasional bit of machinery can be found."[8]

Imhof chronicled eleven ghost towns along the Wild and Scenic section of the Clarion between Ridgway and Hallton. He also accurately observed that "nothing can surpass the experience of actually visiting the sites." This was exactly what I had in mind. Except that my idea of visiting included a canoe, a 12-gauge shotgun, and a box or two of #2 steel shot.

Given our busy schedules, Dan and I agreed to meet at a convenience store off of I-80 the night before our trip, then drive to our campsite. The plan was to drop his truck at the canoe launch at Hallton in the morning, drive my truck with the canoe onboard up to Ridgway, then put in there and float back down. While the drive from Hallton to Ridgway is less than an hour, I figured the float trip would take the better part of the day.

Dan and I pulled into the parking lot within seconds of each other at about 8 PM. After cursory greetings we headed inside to stock the coolers with pop and sandwiches for tomorrow's trip. I told him that if we got set up in time we could stop by the Hallton Hilton, a local bar, for a nightcap. "Sounds good to me," he agreed as we headed out the door.

As we headed north toward the National Forest, we left more and more of the civilized world behind us. First oncoming cars began to dwindle, and soon the soft glow of light from house windows along the road ceased. By the time we crept along the aptly named River Road, an unpaved, sinuous stretch of gravel that parallels the Clarion, the only traffic was the occasional group of deer that couldn't be troubled to move out of our headlight beams.

Thankfully, the campsite I had scoped out earlier was empty. Since we knew our accommodations for the night were available, we headed upriver to the canoe launch where we'd be dropping Dan's truck in the morning. When we reached the narrow parking area, we ran through the estimated departure and arrival times for the morning.

"Alright, then," I concluded, glancing at my watch, "It's only 9:30. Do you want to stop for a brew at the Hallton Hilton on the way back to camp?"

Dan seemed puzzled. "You told me about that place and I was looking for it on the way here, but I didn't see any bar," he said.

"It's just right down there," I answered, pointing back the road we had just driven, "Not even a mile."

"Was that the place with the trucks parked along the road?" he asked with a note of doubt, as though wondering if I was putting him on.

"Yeah," I replied, "The only place we passed that had any signs of life at all."

"I thought that might have been it, but that place just looks like somebody's house," said Dan, still unsure.

"That's the Hilton," I assured him, "Trust me."

I feel the need to explain right here that, if there's one field in which I can claim to be an expert, it's bars. Growing up, I stocked saloon coolers when I was barely strong enough to lift a case of beer and played shortstop on a tavern softball team before I was old enough to drive. During my teen years, my bedroom was located directly above the jukebox of a dive bar, providing a steady subliminal soundtrack of *Sweet Home Alabama* and *Elvira* to all of my dreams. After I reached legal drinking age, let's just say that I opened more than a few bar doors – and closed quite a few of those places too.

The small towns and back roads around the Allegheny are populated with bars like the Hickory Nut Inn, Cougar Bob's, Ridgway Grill, Westline Inn, Grumpy's, and Tack's Inn (which inexplicably sports a sign highlighted by swaying palm trees). But I can honestly say that in all my travels and all my taverns, never have I encountered a bar quite like the Hallton Hilton.

For starters, the Hilton is one of only a handful of structures remaining in Hallton, one of Imhof's ghost towns. Founded around a sawmill in the 1820s, the tiny town at the confluence of Spring Creek and the Clarion River boomed when the lumber ventures of Hall, Gardner and Company sprung up there in the 1880s.[9] Logs were floated down Spring Creek to Hallton's sawmill, where they were ripped into square timber and floated in rafts down the Clarion River to market.

At its peak, the bustling town had stores, a school, a post office, and three churches. But as the trees vanished from the surrounding mountainsides, so too did the residents and businesses of Hallton. The last of the major businesses – a wood chemical plant – closed in 1948 and Hallton today has only a handful of permanent residents. The only other buildings remaining besides hunting camps are, ironically, the Church of Christ and the Hallton Hilton.

The Hilton is housed in what used to be the Grange Hall but, as Dan pointed out, it looks like just an old house. Because there's no parking lot to speak of, just a dirt patch barely big enough for a pair of vehicles to sit side by side, we pulled our trucks off to the side of the road, parking behind a half-dozen others.

We carefully climbed the muddy path to the front porch, lit dimly by a single bulb above the door. As we strolled in, everyone in the place turned an evaluating stare upon us. This didn't take much of an effort since there were only about 10 people in the place, clustered around the bar and two tables.

It's hard to call what's happening inside the Hilton "décor." It appears to be furnished with odds and ends left over from another time, perhaps the closing of the chemical plant six decades ago. Somehow, though, it manages to avoid any sort of antique feel, perhaps by smothering it under several layers of grime. The tile floor, complete with missing sections that reveal tar paper and other unidentified materials beneath, leads to walls covered with paintings of animals. Again, under other circumstances I might be tempted to describe these as murals, but that would convey a feeling of art that doesn't exist here. Using only three colors – black, green, and brown – the paintings are clear enough to convey what they're intended to be (I seem to recall a bear, some deer, and a raccoon), but that's about it. The Hallton Hilton is not strong on nuance.

It is strong on serving beer, though, so I grabbed two and we plopped ourselves at an empty table near the jukebox, which was blaring out '70s rock. The solid black painting of the bear loomed over us. With a final surveying scan around the room, Dan finally pronounced, "Nice place."

I raised my IC Light in a toast to him. "Only the finest when you're with me," I answered with a smile.

Most of the rest of the folks in the place were about what I expected: flannel over stained T-shirts, dented ball caps, heavy on the camouflage. The men were dressed about the same. The table directly behind me, though, stood out. Clustered around it were three twenty-somethings – two guys and a girl – who were sucking down cans of beer like they thought there might be cash at the bottom.

But what caught our attention much more than their drinking habits was the long blonde hair and curving body of the female member of their party. Her scrubbed appearance and upscale clothes – designer jeans and an Aeropostale hoodie – fairly shouted that she wasn't a regular. I pegged her as a college girl from one of the local towns, home to tear it up a little for the weekend.

As our own beers slid down, Dan and I covered the usual range of guy conversation. We grumbled about our wives, griped about work, and speculated on the Steelers' chances for the rest of the season. At one point, I noticed Dan's eyes wandering over my shoulder toward the blonde seated behind me and I followed his gaze with an exaggerated turn of my head. When I turned back to him with raised eyebrows, he just grinned and said, "I think she's digging me."

"Oh, no doubt," I replied reassuringly, "Those 20-year old girls are always looking to hook up with middle aged guys like us, especially when they're already hanging out with a couple of guys their own age."

Perhaps a half-hour later, Blondie wandered past our table to the ladies room, which happened to be located behind Dan's chair. On the way by she flashed me a passably friendly grin, then as Dan scooted his chair to allow her room to pass, she slid her left hand up the side of his chest and onto his shoulder in a motion so slight and effortless that for a moment I wasn't sure it even happened. But when Dan's gaze met mine with a look of mild shock, I knew my eyes hadn't deceived me.

"I guess you weren't bullshitting me," I said, giving him an admiring look.

"Guess not," he answered, half proudly and half sheepishly.

When Blondie returned to her seat without glancing at us, the incident was soon forgotten and we launched again into storytelling. About an hour later she got up for a return visit to the restroom, this time weaving a bit more and ignoring both Dan and me en route.

Then things began to get weird.

One of her companions, a tall, lanky lad with shoulder-length hair and an apparent fear of both combs and shampoo, staggered past us and knocked on the ladies room door. It promptly opened to admit him. Dan's eyes again met mine with a look that said, "What the hell?"

We pondered what would come next, but didn't have to wait long as the ladies room door opened again and Blondie strolled out. Strolled, that is, until she reached the back of Dan's chair, which she proceeded to trip over. As she pitched forward, I instinctively reached out my right arm to stop her momentum and her stomach landed on my forearm.

Without looking at me or speaking, she shuffled back toward her table. I heard a jingling noise and glanced down to see her belt, unbuckled and flapping at her waist.

A few minutes later, her shaggy pal ambled out, looking as if leaving the ladies room was the most normal thing in the world. Then he too tripped over the leg of Dan's chair. While he managed not to fall, he turned to mutter something unintelligible but not very pleasant sounding in Dan's direction.

"What was that?" snapped Dan.

One unfortunate consequence of all the hours I've logged in bars over the years, is that I've also spent a little time around bar fights. And one of the clear signals that a brawl is brewing is often a question like "What did you say?" or "Excuse me?"

Or "What was that?"

It's not normally a question the inquisitor really wants answered. And, depending upon the reply, the next sound is often the fleshy pop of knuckles hitting cheekbone.

Taking stock of the situation, I instantly came to the conclusion that any brawl between Dan and Ladies Room was going to be short, but messy. The younger man was tall, maybe a shade over six feet, but he didn't weigh 175 pounds even with the extra grease in his hair. Dan, on the other hand, is about 5'10" and a solid 190. He had only moments ago finished telling me about his stint in the Marines. Messy indeed.

As Ladies Room lurched around to face Dan, I slid my chair slightly back from the table and glanced back toward Blondie and their other friend. Bar brawl etiquette dictated that my job was to keep the rest of the clientele, especially the other guy at their table, enjoying the show from their seats instead of engaging in any audience participation.

As all of this unfolded in a matter of seconds, a remarkable thing happened. This staggering, sullen guy – who was probably only a few seconds from having Dan scrub the floor of the Hallton Hilton using him as a mop – mustered a last tiny flicker of good judgment.

He looked squarely at Dan, wavered on his feet for a moment, and mumbled, "Nothin'." Then Ladies Room turned and lurched back to his seat.

When Dan and I exchanged looks this time, I know mine was one of relief.

Still, the fun was far from over. By the time we settled back in and half-finished what we determined would be our last round of beer, another commotion broke out at the table of youngsters.

It started with the sound of beer cans toppling, followed by a girl's squeal. I whipped around in time to see the trio headed out the door: the guy who hadn't left the table all night in the lead, followed by Ladies Room with Blondie, laughing herself silly, slung over his shoulder in a fireman's carry.

The few of us left in the room chuckled over the unusual departure, then turned back to our drinks. But about ten minutes later one of the guys at the bar strolled outside then shortly reappeared at the door. The jukebox had shut down for the night, so when he announced, "If that asshole runs into my truck I'm going to kill him," he seemed to be shouting it across the quiet room.

We hadn't considered that the three kids who were too drunk to even walk across the room without navigational problems were now headed outside to steer a course along the dark and narrow River Road...right past our trucks. When I said, "We better settle up and get out of here," Dan nodded quickly in agreement. I paid the tab, ducked into the restroom (despite the trend set earlier in the night, I opted for the men's room), and we moved out the door.

Stepping out into the murky night, we stopped on the narrow porch to let our eyes adjust. I started along the muddy path to the road and about halfway down glanced over my shoulder to tell Dan to watch his step. Turning forward again, I noticed a commotion at the truck parked directly in front of mine. I covered a couple more steps – moving within about 10 feet of the truck – before I finally processed what I was seeing.

There, in the bed of a pickup on the bank of the Clarion River, were Blondie and Ladies Room, *in flagrante delecto*.

Well, OK, that's not technically correct. The *delecto* had either already finished or had never actually occurred because Ladies Room was stretched out next to her on his stomach. Blondie, on the other hand, was reclining stark naked on her back in the truck bed – with the tailgate down, no less. Even in the cloudless murk of the night, her pale thighs seemed to glow white.

Stunned, I slid to a halt and took in the scene. Then, not knowing what else to do, I walked on toward my truck. As I passed the front of their truck, which was facing the front of mine, I encountered the third amigo, bent over the front bumper with his outstretched arms supporting him against the hood.

At first I thought he was throwing up, but as I brushed by him to get into my Ford, I realized he was simply giddy with laughter. He turned to me and said with a cackle, "Everyone's a little drunk tonight."

"Looks like it's working out OK for them," I replied as I unlocked the truck and climbed in.

As I pulled out it occurred to me that this might not be a laughing matter and that this poor girl might be in real trouble. Passing the bed of their truck, I slowed and looked over again, only to see them sitting upright and locked in a passionate kiss. She didn't seem to require any help from me.

When I pulled into our campsite a couple miles down the road, Dan's green Chevy pickup rolled in behind me. I walked back to greet him as he got out.

We stood in the glare of his interior light for a few seconds before I said, "Now there's something you don't see every day."

"Unfortunately!" Dan retorted.

There didn't seem to be much more I could add to that, so we set up our tent and quickly cashed in for the night.

By morning, however, we had new energy and a fresh perspective on the previous night's events. We began breaking them down like post-game football analysts. All we lacked was a telestrator.

"You know," I began, "I was thinking about that girl last night."

"Yeah!" Dan countered quickly, "So was I!"

After a chuckle, I said, "No, really. I was just thinking, it was pretty cold last night. It must've to have been down into the 30s. She had to be freezing in the bed of that truck."

"That must've been why she left her socks on," he replied.

"She did?"

"Yeah, she had socks on."

"I didn't notice," I said. After a few seconds, I added, "Truthfully, I couldn't tell you whether she had feet or not."

That pretty much set the tone for the day. Hardly a ten-minute span went by that didn't contain a reference to naked women or simply the head-shaking observation, "I just can't believe that happened."

Nonetheless, we still had hunting to do. We put in at Ridgway at about 8 AM, just as the morning fog was lifting off the river. After a quick discussion, we agreed that the man in back would paddle while the front man would shoot; we would switch every hour or so. Dan took the shooter's seat first.

We had barely cleared the safety zone downriver from Ridgway when our first birds of the day took wing. Three mergansers that had been tucked in some brush along the left bank of the river suddenly started pulling for the sky about 30 yards downstream. Dan got off two shots at the retreating birds, but neither of us was really prepared for their appearance and they soared downriver unharmed.

Dan was a little unnerved at getting a shot so soon and he was more than a little disappointed at his misses. It didn't help any when a volley of shots came from downriver about two minutes later.

"Well," I said in my most philosophical voice, "if we don't get any ducks, at least we can do some good for the rest of the hunters along the river." It was probably a good thing that I couldn't see his face from the back of the canoe.

We didn't have much time to fret over the miss because five minutes later two more birds, a pair of wood ducks, flashed out of an aspen blowdown that drooped in the water just 25 feet from the left gunwale of the canoe.

Dan swung on the pair, opening up with all three rounds from his Mossberg 935. I waited for one of them to splash into the water, but the splash never came as they too soared down the river valley ahead of us.

Dan's disappointment began to morph into frustration. I'm sure my hilarity at his misses didn't help any.

Still, the early birds were an encouraging start to the morning and our spirits brightened again when we ran into a group of three hunters on a large island. The hunter hidden on the northern point of the island had already shot two wood ducks – probably the two we missed – but the two on the southern tip of the island hadn't had a crack at anything yet. Their young Lab bounded out into the shallow water to visit us for a minute then we were past them and on our way again.

Before we ended our hurried conversation with them, one of the hunters, a young woman, observed, "You guys are doing this the right way. We might get ducks or we might not, but we're just going to be sitting here. You guys are going to hunt ducks and see the whole river too."

We flushed another pair of mallards about 20 minutes later, but they were too far out when Dan fired and the steel shot had no effect. Soon it was time to switch places in the canoe and I enthusiastically took the gunner position. For some reason, though, that seemed to put a stop to the duck sightings, so I filled the time regaling Dan with some of the history of the Clarion's ghost towns.

At the site of Mill Haven, a lumber town that existed only from about 1840 till about 1900, we paddled out of the main channel, behind the ruins of the historic dam, into what used to be the mill pond. In doing so, we were following the same route that tens of thousands of feet of timber floated 150 years ago.[10]

Before railroads, logging was typically done during winter months when fallen trees could be more easily skidded by oxen teams to the banks of a waterway. There the logs were either lashed together into rafts and floated downriver, or stacked on the banks to await high water in the spring.

On the smaller tributaries, "splash dams" were built to push the logs downstream. When the spring rains came and the snow melted, the logs were rolled into the pool above the splash dam. When the water reached sufficient volume, the dam was quickly dropped – splashed – and the timber took off downstream, riding the resultant wave.

Moving logs downriver in loose pieces like this was called a log drive. On larger waterways like the Clarion, dams like the one at Mill Haven were used to force timber from these drives out of the river and into mill ponds where they could be hauled out and sawed into lumber.

The Mill Haven pond today is simply a quiet backwater. It looked like an excellent place for ducks to hide, so Dan and I drifted the Grumman slowly and quietly, hunched over and ready for the splash of wings on the water. To our disappointment, though, there were no birds and we floated out below the dam ruins and back into the river.

Here we received a pleasant surprise as a mature bald eagle sailed off of a mountainside and glided out above us for a minute or two before peeling off and drifting back up the valley. We realized that the eagle's presence was probably the reason that there were no ducks in the Mill Haven pond, but, as he banked against the slate gray sky just a few dozen feet above us, it was a trade we were willing to make.

Just below Mill Haven I pointed out the location of the Idlewild Cut to Dan. Although it's difficult to imagine while bobbing among the shocking reds and oranges of the changing fall foliage today, this huge area of steep hillsides sweeping down to sinuous river curves had, by the end of the 1800s, been cut completely bare. I told Dan of a photo in Imhof's book in which individual rocks can be identified jutting out of the barren hillside. As we drifted out of reach of the Idlewild cut, we silently pondered Nature's power of recovery.

Dan and I switched places again shortly downriver from the Idlewild Cut and it wasn't long until he was blasting away again, this time at a flock of about ten mergansers flushing from below a set of rapids. But because the birds flushed far ahead and because we were still tossing in the shallow rapids, Dan had virtually no chance and the birds flew off around the next bend.

Luckily, they didn't go far and we got another crack at them within an hour. Unluckily, the circumstances were nearly identical and the mergansers once again got away from us and disappeared downriver.

For the next few hours, the same pattern held – with Dan in the bow there seemed to be birds around every other bend in the river; with me in the shooter's spot, we found only the bends. We stopped at Portland Mills, a sort of quasi-ghost town that a few hardy residents stubbornly keep from winking out of existence. They hang on despite the fact that all of the tree-driven industries that once steered the economy of the little hamlet – the lumber mill, the tannery, the matchstick factory, the lath mill, the kindling wood plant – were all gone by 1923, again, victims of a disappearing forest.[11]

At the public canoe launch in Portland Mills, we hogged down our sandwiches and were treated to a grouse buzzing across the river overhead, followed soon after by another bald eagle soaring down the valley. We shoved the canoe back into the river and followed him downstream.

Funny thing about drifting the Wild and Scenic section of the Clarion in a canoe: even with watches and a topo map to gauge our progress, we eventually lost track of both time and place, mesmerized by the flaming foliage on the surrounding slopes and the rhythmic thumping of the paddle on the gunwale. The conversation had slowly ground to a halt; it seemed almost blasphemous to speak in anything louder than a whisper.

That, of course, was before we fell in the river.

Between Portland Mills and Arroyo (yet another of Imhof's ghost towns), we hit the roughest stretch of rapids. With Dan paddling hard in the front, and me shouting directions and paddling just as hard from the stern, we shot through what seemed to be the worst of it only to find our path suddenly blocked by a monstrous boulder.

With no room to maneuver, we rammed up onto the edge of the rock and began to list dangerously to our left. Dan tried to wriggle us free until I noticed our left gunwale, which was only an inch or two above the roiling water. Telling him to freeze, I leaned the other way and shifted some gear, which righted us somewhat, but it turned out to be only temporary.

My fidgeting had freed the stern to move out into the current more and it quickly swung around as the bow stayed put. I thought – prayed – for a second that this would lift us off our rocky perch and send us off downriver again.

Not a chance. As soon as we were exactly perpendicular to the flow of the river, the back of the canoe lodged on another rock and our fate became as clear as the mountain water splashing around us. With the downriver side of the canoe locked front and back, the upriver side rolled underwater in seconds.

Hoping that we could at least keep this from becoming a real disaster, I shouted to Dan over the roar of the water, "Get out! Hold onto the boat!" Into the frigid water we went.

For a few moments, I couldn't speak because the icy shock of the river seemed to suck the very soul out of me. The look on Dan's face and the perfect 'O' formed by his mouth as he tried to find his lungs told me that he was experiencing the same thing.

To make matters worse, we found that we were over a hole in the river where neither of us could touch bottom. And now we had to navigate our half-drowned canoe, along with those contents that hadn't already escaped into the rushing river, across that deep hole to the nearest bank.

The dicey trip covered about 30 slippery, chilly feet. At last, we made it safely to a small eddy near the north bank of the river and began to collect ourselves. I watched my jacket, hunting license still pinned firmly to the back, drift off on the current, but thankfully I had the satisfaction of seeing my $500 video camera, safely sealed in its heavy duty Ziploc bag, bobbing securely along the shore.

After taking account of the sodden contents strewn around the canoe and the riverbank, I said, "Other than my jacket, I think we grabbed everything important. And we'll catch up with the jacket downriver."

"Everything except my gun," returned Dan with a half-chuckle.

"Yeah, right," I laughed back at him.

"I'm serious," he said, looking forlornly at the foaming river. "It was sitting in my lap and when we tipped up it just slid right in."

Unbelievable. We had just gotten out of the current, just recovered from the shock of the spill in the glacial water, and now I knew what had to happen. I was going to have to go back in. This trip was my idea and now it was my fault that Dan's $500 Mossberg 12-gauge was resting somewhere on the bottom of the Clarion River. The 30 feet we had waded and swum through slick boulders and pounding rapids looked more like 30 miles.

Well, I thought, at least I won't get any wetter.

"I'll go get it," I announced and without waiting for an argument, I snagged a life jacket, threw it around my neck, and headed back out into the water.

I made good progress for the first few feet, but I hadn't counted on having to swim even harder against the buoyancy of the life jacket in the frothing water. Stroking and kicking for all I was worth, and battling to hold even an ounce of air in my searing lungs, I managed to get to a spot where I could get a little bit of footing among the slimy boulders.

Once there, I groped for the gun along the river bottom using both hands and feet. There were a couple of false alarms over shotgun-shaped sticks and a couple of stumbles that resulted in rather large and lovely bruises on my legs. It was going to be an impossible task.

And then, astoundingly, I peered down into a dark hole amid the rapids and spied the camouflage finish of Dan's 12-gauge lying peacefully on the bottom. Ducking my head under the water, I pulled it up from the rocky substrate and raised it triumphantly above my head.

"I got it!" I bellowed.

And then, as water poured out of the barrel: "Is it supposed to do that?"

"It didn't do that half an hour ago!" my grinning partner yelled from the bank.

Soon enough we had wrung out everything that could be squeezed and we were back underway. Not far downstream we found my jacket and even recovered a half-full bottle of Mountain Dew that had gone overboard during the tumult.

We still had about two hours of floating ahead of us and luckily we both had clothing on that kept us warm even in our soaked condition: me, a wool shirt and Dan, a Gore-Tex coat. Since my ancient Crescent Arms 12-gauge side-by-side didn't seem any worse for the wear – given its worn condition, it could hardly be made worse – I retook the shooter position in the bow.

Although I hadn't seen a duck from here all day, my luck now seemed to change completely; perhaps I had bought myself some good karma in rescuing Dan's sunken shotgun. Regardless of the reason, I had a half-dozen shots within the next hour. Unfortunately, the dunking didn't seem to do much for my wingshooting skill, so they all turned out to be misses. Still, I found that the sight of mallards and black ducks, along with an occasional flock of mergansers, can warm you as quickly as any campfire.

As we entered the last stretch of our trip, the banks of the river were lined with fishermen and any chance for ducks was long gone. As damp and creaky as we felt after nearly eight hours in the canoe – and a key part of the trip *out* of the canoe – we were still sorry to see Dan's truck come into view at Hallton. Sorry partly because, although we'd seen more than 20 ducks and had more than 50 flushes total, we hadn't bagged one. But also because we didn't want to end the adventure.

We'd gone from ice cold beer to icy river water, from naked women to bald eagles. We'd seen flushing ducks and forgotten towns. And all without leaving the banks of this gorgeous river.

In the end, the Clarion River was just as good as advertised. It really was wild…and scenic.

CHAPTER 4

THE THOUSANDTH ACRE DEER

The area within the boundaries of the Allegheny National Forest is very different today from what its first white explorers found in the middle eighteenth century. Towns now exist where none did before, buildings dot the landscape, and paved roads form a network throughout much of the Forest.

And the forest itself is very different from the woodlands that greeted those first Europeans. Rather than the hemlock and beech trees that towered over the landscape 250 years ago, the mature forest on the Allegheny today is dominated by black cherry, maple, and oak. This is the forest that emerged from the intensive clear-cutting of the late nineteenth and early twentieth century, and survives today under a regimen of forest management and evolving environmental factors such as whitetail deer browsing, acid precipitation, and insect infestations.

There are, however, places on the Allegheny where windows to the ancient forest still exist. The Hearts Content Recreation Area, for example, contains 101 acres of virgin white pine forest, and the Allegheny River Islands Wilderness has a few scattered trees that date to the 1600s. But the largest stand of uncut forest on the Allegheny – in fact, the largest remaining virgin tract between the Adirondack and Smoky Mountains – is the combined 4,131 acres of the Tionesta Scenic Area and Tionesta Research Natural Area.

By the time of the Great Depression, the Tionesta stand stood in stark relief next to the clearcut mountainsides around it. This contrast was highlighted in a 1933 article by Reginald Forbes of the American Forestry Association in which he claimed that "Nine hundred and ninety-nine acres of forest land out of a thousand in the Allegheny territory have been cut over." He then dubbed the virgin timber of the Tionesta tract, "The Thousandth Acre."[12]

Forbes' description of the Tionesta forest is striking: "Here...we felt as though we stood in a gigantic hall, pillared by magnificent hemlock trunks, roofed by canopy above canopy of dark green hemlock needles, and carpeted by five centuries' fall of the same rich fabric...[N]early all the trees were over two feet in diameter, scores were above three feet, and now and then we measured one exceeding four feet...The hardwoods are principally beech, the best with clean boles of such dizzy height and exquisite proportions that I have since speculated whether the pillars of the first Greek temple were not conceived...in a grove of beeches. As for sugar maple, a timber cruiser...told me that day that he had found 'the biggest sugar maple tree in the United States...'"

Forbes also tossed a few overheated words for hunters: "As a hunting ground I dare not describe it, lest my reader take advantage of my indiscretion. Partridge, rabbit, deer, bear had left more tracks in that first snow than I have ever seen in an equal area in the East." He then concluded that "...Tionesta Forest has a value so far beyond that which may be derived from its conversion into lumber, tan bark, and chemical wood that it is unutterably tragic to think of its passing."[13]

Other members of the forestry community agreed and, inspired in part by Forbes glowing descriptions of the Tionesta tract, undertook an effort to have the virgin stand incorporated into the Allegheny National Forest. The purchase was approved and the Tionesta tract was added to the Allegheny in 1936.

The total price tag was roughly $750,000 for the 4,000 acres of uncut timber within the Tionesta tract and an additional 12,000 acres of land that had previously been cut. Doing the math, it seems that one of the most valuable and rare ecological sites in the East was acquired for about $47 an acre.

In a Solomonic decision reflecting the "Land of Many Uses" motto of the National Forest, half of this unique resource was designated for low impact recreational use and the other half was dedicated to scientific study. Both areas were named as National Natural Landmarks in 1973.

Dr. Susan L. Stout, Research Project Leader at the USFS Forestry Sciences Laboratory since 1991, explains that the Tionesta RNA is a focal point of scientific study on the Allegheny because it provides an arena for study in a centuries-old ecosystem that can't be recreated. Among the many findings in over six decades of study is that much of the hemlock in the Tionesta dates to about 1550, while the oldest individuals have survived for more than 500 years.

Stout notes, though, that the administrative protection given to the tract essentially precludes any kind of damage to trees, even for scientific study. "For the most part, any kind of manipulation is out of the question," she says of the Tionesta, but adds, "One of the ironies of that is that there can be human-caused influences that have a huge impact on the Tionesta – things like acid rain and especially the choices that people make in regard to management of deer populations."

Ah, yes, deer populations. Strictly from a selfish perspective, I was excited when I picked up a copy of the Allegheny National Forest Hunting Map and saw that my prospective whitetail hunting spots – both the Tionesta Scenic Area and RNA – were marked with an "H" for "High Deer Density." This designation, which indicates areas with more than 30 deer per square mile, is the maximum indicated on the map.

Stout does not share my enthusiasm for the high number of deer on the Tionesta since when their presence is wrecking the normal processes that would keep these National Natural Landmarks healthy. She describes "theoretical old growth" as a scenario in which individual trees die and are replaced by those that have grown below the canopy. "You have to have conditions that allow trees to replace themselves in the understory," she states. However, "the current understory conditions are completely dictated by deer densities," which interferes with the replacement process. "Up to two years ago I literally never saw a hemlock seedling over two inches tall out there," she says sadly.

To correct the situation, the USFS has enlisted the help of hunters. To bring the herd into balance with its environment, they're encouraging hunters to harvest more antlerless deer and making additional antlerless licenses available to enable that. "They're critical," said Stout of deer hunters at the Tionesta tract. "Hunting is absolutely essential to achieve our management objectives when it comes to deer."

The challenge is that a 4000-acre, largely roadless tract characterized by rugged slopes and massive blowdowns may not be every hunter's cup of tea. Stout acknowledges as much, but asserts that, "There's an opportunity to market it as a wilderness hunting experience. I think there's also a chance to attract a specific community of hunters, those with a certain stewardship ethic who would welcome the opportunity to make a contribution [to protecting the ecology of the Tionesta tract]."

She had found such a hunter in yours truly. Although Pennsylvania's October muzzleloader season for antlerless deer allows a variety of ignition systems, including modern in-lines, I prefer to do my front stuffing the old-fashioned way – with a patch and a ball and flint striking steel. My rifle of choice is a Pennsylvania Long Rifle replica because, as an eighth generation Pennsylvanian, I like to imagine I'm strolling the woodlands as my ancestors did over 250 years ago.

The Tionesta tract seemed like a place where I could enjoy a backwoods experience and do my civic duty at the same time. It would be a terrific spot to let my imagination run – though truthfully it never strayed too far from the big, black "H" on that map.

I had barely dried out from duck hunting on the Clarion when I found myself staring down the iron sights of my long rifle at a paper target. The day before muzzleloader season opened, I put five shots in a 4-inch ring at 100 yards despite a heavy crosswind and intermittent bursts of rain. When the final shot nicked the edge of the bull's-eye, my confidence soared.

That evening I was in the Ford and headed north. I had a place to stay within a half-hour drive of the Tionesta since fellow biologist Ken Stockert generously offered the use of his camp. I later graciously repaid Ken's kindness by horning in on both bear and deer hunting at Camp Stockert – thus allowing him to graduate from business acquaintance to hunting buddy, a far nobler distinction.

The alarm at camp went off at 5:45 AM, and I was up and out quickly. At 7 AM I rolled into the Tionesta entrance road, which roughly marks the boundary between the RNA and the Scenic Area. The pre-dawn drizzle had given up, replaced by a menacingly black morning sky. The first snow of the year was forecasted for later that night. I loaded the rifle with a 75-grain charge, tucked a topo map into my vest, and headed south in search of big timber and a big doe.

My plan for the day was not complicated. I would walk southeast along the plateau into the headwaters of West Fork Run, and then crest the next ridge into the East Fork Run valley. Once on the East Fork, I would meander downstream until I found a deer. Since the streams were essentially parallel and there was only one mapped road within the Tionesta tract it would make navigation easy. Or so I thought.

When I came to the path shown on my map I was surprised to find that it was actually a somewhat improved dirt road and I soon discovered that it led to an active oil well. This was also a surprise given the restrictions on this area, but I reasoned that perhaps I wasn't quite over the border into the Tionesta RNA yet.

Just past the oil well, the road dissolved into a field of goldenrod and ferns. It was loaded with deer sign: fresh tracks, recent droppings, and matted beds.

I was positive I was within the RNA now, but there was still no big timber here. Disappointed at the lack of giant hemlocks and beech, I was also now encountering a bigger problem – the terrain wasn't doing what I expected. I thought I should have reached the rim of the West Fork basin by now, but I was still walking along the flat top of the plateau. After mulling it over for a bit, I decided to consult the map to refresh my memory.

Planting myself on a conveniently downed cherry tree trunk in a small clearing, I leaned the rifle against the downed tree and fished the map out of my vest pocket. I stared intently, retracing my route on paper and trying to pinpoint my location. I was so focused, in fact, that it took me a few seconds to realize that there was a deer walking through the woods to my right.

By the time I saw the mature doe she was no more than 25 yards away and moving at a leisurely pace. I rapidly calculated that her path would bring her into the clearing almost directly in front of me.

I was now faced with a couple of problems. First, I was probably going to need a gun in the very near future and I didn't have one in my hands at the moment. Second, what I *was* holding in my hands, an inconveniently large green and white topographic map, did not seem to be an effective choice as a weapon, but had exceptional possibilities when it came to frightening away an approaching deer. In fact, the upper left corner of the map was now flapping slightly in the stiffening breeze.

Before I could decide how to resolve this situation, the big shouldered doe stepped into the clearing. To my amazement, she stopped broadside about 30 yards from my seat and started to munch on the grass near her feet. There wasn't a stick of cover between us. She was close enough that I could see the ruffles in her dark coat, still wet from last night's rain.

My heart hammered a calypso beat against my ribs. As gently and quietly as possible I tried to dispose of the map by tucking it under my left leg. Each brush of the paper against my pants sounded like an air horn to my ears, but the doe never flinched.

Now, with the map safely stowed, I had to do the reverse with my gun. I grabbed the barrel and gradually tugged it skyward – Why does this damn barrel have to be so damn long? – without taking my eyes off the deer. In subatomic increments I gradually swung the stock toward my body then up to my shoulder. Finally, the brass butt plate snug on my shoulder, I eased back the hammer.

The click of the set trigger didn't cause so much as a twitch of her ear. I dropped the sights in line and set them four inches behind her left shoulder. She stood still, completely unaware. I pulled the trigger.

Through the haze of smoke I saw the big doe buck like a bronco, take two steps forward, then wheel 180 degrees and bolt back down the trail. I could only see her form through the thick brush for about 40 yards, but on the thick morning air I heard her uneven, clomping hoof beats well beyond that. I listened closely to hear her fall, but she was tougher than I hoped and the sound of her running drifted off into the forest.

No matter, I thought, that was a clean shot. Just like that, I had killed a deer on The Thousandth Acre. It was 7:45 AM.

Confident that she would quickly expire, I waited 15 minutes so as not to push her further than necessary. At 8:00 exactly, I got up from my perch, reloaded, and walked to the spot where she stood when I shot. I couldn't find any blood or hair among the sedges and ferns, but I attributed that to their height and density. I waited at that spot for a few minutes longer, feeling vaguely disappointed that I hadn't even made it into the virgin timber yet my hunt was over. But with the sky turning a darker shade of gray and seeming to sink to a level just above my head, I decided it was time to pick up the trail of the deer.

As I passed through the band of thick saplings along the forest edge I realized I was moving into an area of ancient timber. Huge hemlock snags and a few dead beech giants loomed above me with mature cherries and maples filling the gaps where the older trees had died.

With the mid-October leaves still on the hardwoods and the shadows thrown by the few remaining hemlocks, the woods were so dark that I had to turn on my flashlight. When I pulled it from my vest, I was upset to find the ground covered with fallen red maple leaves – blood red maple leaves. Trailing my doe was not going to be as easy as I had hoped.

For 30 or 40 yards I was able to follow the trail of leaves that she had kicked up, but I still couldn't find any blood. Then, at a blown-over beech tree that was at least three feet in diameter, the trail split, with fresh tracks in both directions. Without a blood trail to follow, my confidence began to seep away. It ebbed further when I found that one of the trails traveled out over the rim of the West Fork basin – the spot I had been searching for when the doe surprised me – and into a mass of eight-foot tall black birch trees, every one with its leaves still on, forming a thick curtain of vegetation.

When I ventured a few feet off of the trail to look for the downed deer, I realized that I couldn't even make out my knees, let alone my feet. She could be lying ten feet away, I thought in despair, and I'd never even see her. That's about the time it started to rain.

For the next hour and a half, I swept that ridge and the flat ground above it searching in vain for the downed doe. I returned several times to the spot where I had shot her, circling out in widening arcs, but still found no sign of a blood trail.

As I hunted for any small clue to her whereabouts, I replayed the shot again and again, and slowly began to wonder if I had missed. Maybe I had flinched, pulled the trigger a second too soon. Perhaps I had somehow fired beneath her chest and blown an easy shot. The steady drizzle kept up.

At a little before 10, I gave up the search in disgust, turning back to my original game plan of crossing West Fork Run. In actuality though, I strayed too far east and missed the West Fork entirely, arriving instead in the headwaters of the East Fork – a fact I didn't realize until I examined a newer map weeks later. Here I was surprised again to find roads cleared and trees cut within the RNA.

Further down the valley, I crossed the stream into a solid stand of hemlock that had virtually no vegetation less than six feet tall, a clear indicator of deer damage. Deliberately avoiding the roads and cut areas so that I could soak up some of the true nature of The Thousandth Acre, I continued downstream. After stealthily walking a mile or so through the intermittent rain, I stopped and gazed up.

I was surrounded by giants.

For perhaps a half-hour I simply sat and admired the monster trees around me. Most of them were at least four centuries old, sprouting from the soft, damp forest floor before the Pilgrims landed at Plymouth Rock, before John Smith met Pocahontas. The truly ancient ones among them may have pre-dated Columbus. It was enough to make me feel small, both literally and figuratively.

Upon closer inspection, the Tionesta forest reminded me of an elephant graveyard. Scattered between the living leviathans were at least as many windblown tree corpses, their skeletal remains stretched out across the forest floor. Nearly all of the standing beech appeared to suffer from beech bark disease, which meant that they might soon be joining their dead brothers. With no replacements growing in, I couldn't feel good about the future of The Thousandth Acre.

When my reverie ended, I still-hunted downstream for about an hour, but the going was extremely tough. With frequent three-foot diameter downed trunks to clamber over, it was impossible to move quietly, even on the damp forest floor.

As I crept along my thoughts returned to that morning's deer. I began to rerun the shot in my mind, parsing out the sight picture, the doe's reaction at the shot, and the clumsy sound of her gait as she ran off. With each passing moment I became more and more certain that I had not missed. In fact, I knew it, as surely as I knew the feel of the rifle in my hands.

The more convinced I became, the more agitated I felt until I wasn't really still-hunting anymore, just walking. And each step was taking me further from where a deer – my deer – was lying dead in the forest. The sky was clearing a bit and maybe, I reasoned, more light would help the search. Finally, perhaps three miles downstream from where I started, I decided to go back and find her.

Rather than retracing my difficult steps uphill, I turned north and headed straight up the ridge, figuring it would be quicker to climb the relatively tame hillside here to the road my map said would take me back.

Fifteen minutes after I committed to this route the rain started to pour in earnest. Without a puff of wind, it cascaded like a waterfall over the entire forest. This did little to ease my agitation.

Nor did hiking up the ridge. Hauling my rifle – Why does this damn barrel have to be so damn heavy? – and now soaked to the skin, I was soon wheezing like a locomotive as I crawled, skidded, and stumbled uphill over one massive blowdown after another.

Finally, drenched, drained, and irritated, I reached the top of the ridge and found the road. I turned right and headed to where I hoped I would find my prize waiting. I had covered maybe a quarter-mile when, to my surprise, the road quite suddenly ended at an oil well. Clearly, this was not the main road that I was looking for. Once again, my annoyance was not diminished.

Consulting the topo map was now out of the question because A) it didn't show the road I was on, and B) it now resembled a spitball that I once threw against the chalkboard in seventh grade music class. I had zero desire to fight my way back down the rugged hillside, so I turned and headed in the opposite direction on the road. I knew this was the wrong way, but it was the only path out. At least the monsoon was still raging. That was a nice touch.

I followed one dirt road after another for the next hour-plus, always trying to work my way east, and always finding a dead-end at a well and having to retrace my steps. I was no stranger to drilling on the National Forest, but what were all these well roads doing in the RNA?

"That is a very good question," said Allegheny National Forest biologist Brad Nelson when I posed it to him months later. "I'd rather they weren't there."

"When the original [Allegheny National] Forest purchase was made," explained Nelson, "They didn't acquire the mineral rights. As a result, something like 93 percent of all the mineral rights on the Forest are privately held."

He elaborated that there wasn't much interest in gas and oil on the Tionesta tract until the late 1960s. "When they decided to drill we had to give them access to their wells," said Nelson. "We didn't like it but there wasn't much we could do about it." And thus, in a few sentences, did Nelson sum up one of the most furious controversies surrounding the Allegheny National Forest.

In 1859, just a few miles southwest of the current boundary of the Allegheny National Forest, Col. Edwin Drake drilled a 70-foot hole in the forest floor and created the world's first producing oil well. This discovery simultaneously started a new industry and ignited a change in technology and transportation that still shapes our world a century and a half later.

Drake's revolution has also come to define many of the conflicts in our modern world. Wars are fought over the control of oil resources worldwide while here in the US, the most vocal and contentious environmental disputes surround fossil fuels, most notably access on public land. With the ongoing controversy over oil drilling in Alaska's Arctic National Wildlife Refuge ringing in the nations' ears, a similar scenario is also playing out in the northwestern corner of the Keystone State.

There are more than 6,000 active oil and gas wells on the Allegheny today. Of course, the companies producing these have every right to their resource and each barrel of oil or volume of natural gas they produce in Pennsylvania is another we don't have to pay another country for. Taking that a step further, these domestic fuel sources might eventually reduce our need to put soldiers in harm's way in the Middle East. As one local said to me, "Every bit of it they produce here might bring one more soldier home from over there."

Unsurprisingly, anti-development groups don't see it that way. The level of mineral extraction on the Allegheny – along with the active timber management on the Forest – led the National Forest Protection Alliance to identify this National Forest in 2001 as their "Most Endangered National Forest." It made their Top 10 list once again in 2003. They would apparently prefer the motto "Land of a Relatively Few Uses."

Another group chiming in on drilling on the Allegheny is The Wilderness Society. In their *Energy and Public Lands Report*, this national wilderness advocacy group specifically addressed the Tionesta tract, noting that "[w]ells, pipelines and roads punctuate the landscape surrounding the old growth, and can even be found within the boundaries of the area." According to this report there were 120 oil and gas wells present in the Tionesta in June 2000.[14]

However, Nelson told me that there are now just 14 active wells within the RNA and, due to the efforts of a local conservation group, no more will be drilled there. Twenty years ago, the Western Pennsylvania Conservancy, like the National Forest Protection Alliance and The Wilderness Society, were concerned with the growing impact of oil and gas drilling within the RNA. But rather than just shouting solutions from the sideline, the Conservancy came up with a solution.

According to Ann Sand, Assistant Director of Land Protection for the Western Pennsylvania Conservancy, their organization "became involved in a very complex land transaction that required two years of negotiations to stop the development associated with drilling in this important natural area." The deal, which was consummated in 1987, involved the swap of $1 million in oil, gas, and mineral rights at a site in Nevada along with cash, land, and timber rights. In turn, the oil company retained operating rights to their existing wells within the RNA until they are exhausted, at which time they "will be plugged, and associated roads and utilities abandoned".[15]

The purchase agreement did not include the adjoining Tionesta Scenic Area and according to Nelson, the oil, gas, and mineral rights within that area remain private. The WPC's Sand was unwilling to divulge whether her organization is pursuing the acquisition of these rights, citing the risk of driving up the purchase price if such information became public.

The real problem I faced while wandering around the Tionesta RNA obviously wasn't oil well development on its fringes. It was the fact that I had armed myself with an outdated map. And now even that was reduced to a soggy, lumpy pulp so I was left navigating from memory. I couldn't even plot a course by the position of the sun since it was completely shielded behind the opaque wall of iron-gray clouds.

After more than an hour and a half of walking, it was actually a gas pipeline that saved me. When I bumbled out of the maze of access roads onto the pipeline right of way, I realized I'd seen it on my map earlier and that it pointed the way back. In a moment captured directly from the mind of a B-movie director, the sky suddenly cleared and the rain stopped just as I stepped onto the right of way. All that was missing was an angelic chorus.

Somewhat less disgusted now that I knew where I was, I set out to find my deer. Despite being tired, wet, and a long way from where I wanted to be, my pace quickened as the image of the doe standing in the field, the shot, and her reaction ran on a continuous loop through my head. I was positive now. I was going to find her. I did not miss.

It was late afternoon by the time I reached the downed cherry tree in the clearing. Nearly eight hours after I took the shot, I was once again confident and inspired to find the doe that I knew was lying dead in these woods. Although the air had begun to turn chilly, the light was far better than it had been that morning and I set out briskly, almost cheerfully, to track down my prize.

I started by retracing her trail from where she was shot, once again following until it petered out at the same spot. Recognizing that any blood trail had long since been washed away, I opted to search in a methodical grid pattern, widening eventually to about 200 yards from where I shot her.

Another hour soon passed and I still had not even a single piece of evidence to go on. My second wind of enthusiasm was slowly replaced by a following gale of disgust, until finally I succumbed. Head down in the gray dusk, I wandered back to the truck.

The three-hour drive home allowed plenty of time to dry out and think about the disappointments of the day. Aside from losing my deer, I couldn't shake the image of the virgin timber forest as a boneyard where the last giants struggled valiantly against joining fallen comrades at their feet.

Asked later for her vision of the future of the climax forest, Dr. Stout suggested a couple of possibilities. In the bleakest of these deer browsing and beech bark disease continue to prevent native beech trees from reaching maturity and the wooly adelgid, an insect pest that has up to 100 percent mortality on hemlock stands, moves into the Tionesta forest. In this case, Stout says, "We could end up with no hemlock at all and 1" to 8" diameter beech trees constantly cycling through growth then disease." The climax forest would be gone – permanently.

In the best case scenario, disease-resistant beech trees begin to take hold, the wooly adelgid finds that it can't live in the frosty elevations of the Allegheny, and hunters and scientists come together to lower deer densities to a point that allows a more normal forest succession to take place. "Some pretty dramatic changes could be down the pike," concludes Stout, "And much of it depends on the choices to be made, like deer management or whether we introduce another exotic to eliminate the adelgid."

I mulled the fact that that the irreplaceable Tionesta ecosystem is already two steps down the worst case scenario path, and that reversing it toward the best case would require not only levels of cooperation that have never been achieved previously, but also a lot of plain old good luck. It spelled an uncertain future for a national landmark and I doubted whether the course could be corrected. In fact, there was really only one thing that I knew for sure.

I did not miss.

CHAPTER 5

PHEASANTS ON THE FOREST

My consternation over the future of the Thousandth Acre was soon offset by optimism for another Allegheny National Forest spot, one locally known as the Beanfield. My hopefulness came from a conversation with John Mack, who is looking to write a new chapter in the story of the Beanfield. That's no small challenge considering that the documented history of the site goes back more than 10,000 years.

Mack, the founder and president of the Warren County Pheasants Forever chapter, has had his eye on the 300-acre Beanfield, one of the largest open field tracts on the entire Allegheny National Forest, for several years. A longtime Ruffed Grouse Society member, Mack was increasingly discontented that legal action against the USFS was preventing habitat projects on the Allegheny. As a 1997 lawsuit filed by a consortium of local and national organizations including the Allegheny Defense Project and the Sierra Club plodded through federal court, a moratorium was placed on all logging across the Allegheny, and habitat management activities for grouse and woodcock ground to a halt. While RGS proceeded with successful habitat projects at other locations across the US and Canada, Mack fumed over the bureaucratic and legal processes that kept him participating in work here on the Forest he calls home.

Rather than sulking, Mack decided to take his love of upland hunting in a different direction and formed the Warren County PF chapter. In a state where wild pheasant populations have declined very nearly to the point of nonexistence, the densely wooded hills and valleys of Pennsylvania's only National Forest is one of the least likely places for ringneck restoration. But then Mack has a history of combining his interest in the Allegheny National Forest with other facets of his life.

"When I first met my wife, we were in college at Penn State," said Mack, who grew up in a suburb of Pittsburgh. "She told me she was from Pittsfield, but that didn't mean much to me so I dragged out a map to see where it was. When I found it on the map [just west of the ANF], I said, 'You live that close to the National Forest?' She didn't think much about it, but I said to myself, I'm not going to let this one get away." True to his word, Mack married Janet and moved to Warren County. They eventually settled in the tiny village of Dunns Eddy, within spitting distance of Allegheny River and walking distance of the National Forest.

The part of the Forest that lies closest to the Mack household contains two significant National Forest resources: Dr. Susan Stout's Forest Lab and Buckaloons, which includes the Beanfield. The Forest Lab has played a key role in Allegheny National Forest management over the past century. Buckaloons and the Beanfield, on the other hand, played a significant role for the 90 centuries before that.

Buckaloons is the name earliest European explorers gave to the Indian village that they found near the confluence of Brokenstraw Creek and the Allegheny River. The earliest description of the village comes from French explorer Celeron de Bienville during his 1749 journey through the region. After floating Conewango Creek then down the Allegheny River, Celeron held a council with the (mostly Seneca) Indians at Buckaloons to inform them that he was claiming the surrounding country for the French crown.

Although he selected this location for his grand pronouncement, Celeron's journal refers to it as a rather insignificant village. USFS Forest Archaeologist and Forest Heritage Program Manager Rick Kandare, however, vehemently disagrees.

Kandare fairly gushed when I asked about Buckaloons. "That site has 10,000 years of prehistory, not to mention important ties to North American settlement, logging, raft building, and other industry within our recorded history." As evidence, Kandare points out that the precursors to today's archaeological work at Buckaloons include a Smithsonian Institution excavation in the late 1800s.

Kandare is also fond of quoting internationally known archaeologist Verna Cowin, who once told a group of visiting historians that, if she were given the choice of saving either the Liberty Bell or Buckaloons, she would definitely choose the latter. Her reasoning, says Kandare, was sound. "It's a veritable time capsule of human occupation of the North American continent. You have everything that represents prehistory as well as recent history."

In what Kandare calls "10,000 years in 10 minutes," he gave me a brief overview of human settlement across the area that now includes the Allegheny National Forest.

Paleo-Indians emerged between 10,000 and 8,000 B.C., as the glaciers receded and mammoths and saber-toothed tigers roamed the continent. Buckaloons shows archaeological evidence of a rare permanent village from this prehistoric period of human habitation. Why these earliest settlers selected this location hasn't really been answered, but Kandare postulates that the combination of available water transportation, a flat area for settlement, and the confluence of major Indian trails became the foundation of settlement that would stretch for eons.

From the Archaic Period (8,000 to 4,000 B. C.) through the Woodland Period (4,000 B.C. up to European contact), Buckaloons and the Beanfield were part of a whole series of villages along the Allegheny River. The Late Woodland Period, which stretched into the 1790s and included Celeron's visit, saw the ascendance of the Seneca Nation in this area.

Part of the Five Nations of the Iroquois Confederacy, the Senecas were the figurative western door of the Iroquois longhouse – a reference to Iroquois wooden buildings that resembled modern Quonset huts. The Iroquois Confederacy looked upon its geographic reach (from eastern New York to western Pennsylvania) as one large longhouse made up of its member tribes.

By the 1790s, through a convoluted series of treaties and bloody defeats at the hands of English – and later, Americans –the Seneca were moved out of Buckaloons and onto a small reservation on the New York-Pennsylvania line. But the history of habitation at Buckaloons and the Beanfield didn't end at that point.

In 1797, Callendar Irvine received a grant of land near Warren from his father, Brigadier General William Irvine, commander of the Western Department of the US Army. The tract the younger Irvine received was a wide, flat floodplain near the confluence of Brokenstraw Creek and the Allegheny River where an Indian village called Buckaloons had once been situated. Callendar, a son of Scotch-Irish settlers from County Fermanagh, Ireland, quickly turned the fertile tract into an agricultural venture known as Brokenstraw Farm.[16]

When General Irvine died on July 29, 1804, Callendar was tabbed to succeed him as Superintendent of the Military Stores of Philadelphia, and Brokenstraw Farm was left behind. It wasn't until about 35 years later that Callendar's son, William Armstrong Irvine, returned to the forests of Pennsylvania's northwest and re-established the family farm. Soon a small town sprung up, which William named Cornplanter in honor of a great Seneca chief.

Kandare relates that the town's tiny church, which remains today, was built by William as a private chapel for his wife, Sarah Duncan Irvine. Now known as the First Presbyterian Church, or simply "The Little Stone Church," it has a tragic history.

"She refused to move here at first, into what she thought was an untamed wilderness," Kandare says. "So he offered to build her the church, which to her represented civilization and culture."

The young wife consented and the family moved to Cornplanter. However, shortly after their arrival, Sarah died while giving birth to her second daughter. She was just 25 years old. Her funeral was the first service ever held in the Little Stone Church.

The residents of Cornplanter (later renamed Irvine) dabbled in a number of ventures, including a grist mill, logging and, of course, the Irvine family farm. The hundreds of acres of rich soil near the river were planted in a number of crops over the years, including corn and potatoes, but one particular crop left the spot with its distinctive name – the Beanfield.

Today, even after more than a century of investigations and excavations, the Beanfield is still serving up thousands of artifacts. Kandare says that the site still merits intensive investigation, but also requires "a lot of pondering" because its long history of settlement results in "features inside of features inside of features."

From a scientific standpoint, the bottom line on Buckaloons and the Beanfield is straightforward. Although many people prefer the simplistic notion that it was once an untamed, uninhabited forest, in Kandare's words, "one never had wilderness at Buckaloons. Ever since the last Ice Age that site has been used, occupied, and manipulated by humans."

That is exactly the legacy that John Mack would like to tap once again. Shortly after the Warren County PF chapter was formed in 2003, four members got together on a November Saturday morning to chase some of the PGC's stocked birds. As Mack recalls, "It was a little crowded but we had my three labs, plus another one running the Beanfield. It was really a great, fun day. We had birds going all over the place." By 9:30 AM, with the frost barely gone from the tips of the goldenrod, all four men had their two-bird limit.

"It was really a good way for us to come together, a good way to bond the group," says Mack. "But when we were done we started to ask ourselves, 'What can we do to make this place even better?'"

One of Mack's first calls was to USFS public relations representative Mary Hosmer. "We told Mary that we were having some good times down at the Beanfield," he says today, "but the habitat isn't that great for pheasants. We asked if there was some way we could do a project out there." A conservation champion in her own right, Hosmer's first response was to join the PF chapter, but efforts to initiate a habitat project at the Beanfield were torpedoed, ironically by the same legal moratorium that had stymied Mack's earlier RGS efforts.

Hosmer, though, is at least as persistent as Mack. A year later, Mack's phone rang and Hosmer was on the other end with an offer. "She had run the project by the Forest Service again," recalls Mack, "and they bought into it that time."

In actuality, Hosmer had not only convinced the USFS, but also captured donations from RGS and the National Wild Turkey Federation, and nailed down additional cooperative services from the PGC. The PGC would prep the site by planting buckwheat. Then, with $2,500 apiece from PF, RGS, and NWTF, a total of 112 acres of brood rearing and feeding habitat for upland game birds would be planted, consisting mostly of warm season grasses.

On a more recent November morning, over eggs and home fries at nearby Richard's Restaurant, Mack and fellow PF member Scott Blum revealed to me how this project was just the first step in their diabolical plans for domination of the world – or at least the Brokenstraw Valley.

"We see the Beanfield as the centerpiece," explained Mack between sips of coffee, "of a much bigger habitat network stretching up along the Brokenstraw Creek. There is already some really good habitat in the valley and we've already been supplying seed to a couple of farmers there to get some warm season grasses going. We'd like to build a mosaic of pheasant habitat stretching along the entire valley."

"With the Beanfield right at the center of that," Blum chipped in.

"Hunters already know that the Game Commission stocks pheasants there," Mack picked up again, "so they know it now as a pheasant destination, at least for stocked birds. But we'd like to show them that, if you build good habitat there, the Beanfield could actually support a decent *reproducing* pheasant population."

"Not just stocked birds," echoed Blum.

Mack then divulged the next phase of the scheme. "We'd like to use the Beanfield as an educational site too. When we're trying to get private landowners interested in our habitat programs, that'd be a perfect place to take them. We'd be able to not just talk about what habitat could be created, but actually take them out there and show them, point to it."

"Even take them for a hunt there?" I ventured.

"Absolutely," beamed Mack, seeing that I was getting the message. "Definitely. Anything to get their interest and get them involved in the programs."

From the restaurant, we headed west to a state game land for a quick morning hunt while we waited for the crowds at the Beanfield to thin a bit. Mack said that, while the Beanfield doesn't yet attract much attention from outside the area, it does draw a lot of local "truck chasers" who know where and when the PGC stocks ringnecks.

I turned Hunter loose and then had the extreme pleasure of spending an hour and a half watching him hunt with Mack's chocolate Lab, Eddy, and Blum's black Lab, Hank.

Unfortunately, despite all the good dog work, with Hunter working close as always and Eddy and Hank cutting a wake 20 yards further out, all we had to show for it was two hen flushes and a couple of bounding white-tailed deer. Still, we knew that the main event at the historic Beanfield lay ahead.

We parked a few hundred yards south of the Beanfield, directly in front of the last remnant of the once magnificent Irvine Estate. Known locally as 'The Old Stone House,' the official name of the building is the Irvine House in the Pines, which is appropriate considering that it's located within a stand of 200-year old hemlock and white pine. Mack switched dogs to give his black Lab, Izzy, a run.

Looking out across the Beanfield's weedy expanse for the first time, I felt the touch of 10,000 years of history. But before I could ponder it, Mack hustled me to a location by the riverbank and announced, "This is the spot right here. This is where they're going to be planting the warm season grasses next spring. It doesn't look like much right now, but we're hoping it will really turn into something special."

As Izzy, Hank, and Hunter bounded off ahead, the sky turned blacker and the clouds sank down over our ears. The morning was unseasonably warm and the air was so humid that it felt like we were wading through it. At one point, I glanced over at Blum as he paused to wipe sweat from his face. "It's like hunting in Africa," he grimaced.

Since the dogs weren't finding birds, our discussion turned to some of the successes and difficulties that the new chapter was facing. Mack's personal favorite subject, the Youth Pheasant Hunt, came up immediately.

"It was fantastic!" gushed Mack. "We held the first one two years ago and we thought it went pretty well, but this year's outdid that one. As far as I'm concerned, it's the highlight of our year." Mack explained that the PGC provides free birds based upon the number of young hunters registered, but some of the chapter members wanted to go the extra mile. "Some of us chipped in from our own pockets – not chapter money – and bought extra birds from a local supplier for the kids to hunt," he said with a smile.

"They're learning to hunt, which helps us. They're learning that we can have pheasants here in the Beanfield, which may help us with support of our projects in the future. But most importantly, they're learning that shooting a bird isn't just the result of a stocking truck. They can start to understand that if you steward the land a little bit, you can see the results in the field."

Hosmer was on hand at the Youth Hunt to handle the registration, proving again that there really is something about Mary. Mack told the story of a boy in his early teens that showed up at the event without registering. When Hosmer couldn't find his name on the list, his disappointment was so obvious that, rather than turning him away, she turned him over to Mack. In the capable hands of the chapter president and his trusty Labs, the young man shot his limit of two birds. "He was thrilled to death," Mack told me later, his voice deepening with emotion.

Our day in the Beanfield effectively ended about noon when the atmosphere finally exceeded its water capacity and a massive downpour ensued. We pretended to be hunting on the way back to the trucks, but it was barely more than a controlled retreat. We quickly said our goodbyes and dove into our dry vehicles.

Driving home, I thought about Mack and his attempts to add his own chapter to the history of the Beanfield. He and the Warren County PF chapter are staring down ten millennia of human habitation, chasing ghosts of pioneer settlers, and bucking Forest Service red tape to return to nature land that has been tilled for two centuries. It may take years more before he can leave the mark of his personal conservation ethic on the National Forest that he loves.

But succeed or fail, one thing was as clear as the raindrops falling from a November sky. Mack will pursue this goal with passion.

CHAPTER 6

THE FOREST FOR THE TREES

"I was awakened by our alarm service at about 5 AM on August 11, 2002. By the time I got to the building, the fire department was already there and the flames were coming up through the roof."

Dr. Susan Stout's chilling words recall the first few minutes of one of the most malicious events in the history of the Allegheny National Forest – the arson attack on the Forest Research Laboratory in Irvine.

The notorious ecoterrorist group Earth Liberation Front was apparently behind the assault, which, according to Stout, caused damage in the ballpark of $1 million. In an email claiming responsibility for the arson, ELF asserted that the attack on the Forest Lab was made "in response to the threats posed to life in the Allegheny Forest by proposed timber sales, oil drilling, and greed-driven manipulation of nature." They also threatened that "Forest Service administration and research facilities, as well as all DNR buildings nationwide should now be considered likely targets."

Some, including US Congressman John Peterson, a five-term Republican whose district includes the Allegheny National Forest, felt that the Allegheny Defense Project was partly responsible for the arson as well. "World terrorists are against our economic system," Peterson said of ADP, one of the most vociferous and energetic anti-logging and anti-drilling groups, "and in reality, these people are too – they want the Earth for the critters without human involvement."[17]

Ryan Talbott, Forest Watch Coordinator for ADP, took careful steps to distance the organization from the arson, saying that his group has never had any contact with ELF, either before or after the arson. "It was a horrible action and we certainly do no support those kinds of actions," Talbott told me.

While that may be true, ADP does have connections to other militant environmental groups and a history of aggressive acts against Forest Service property. In May 1998, ADP supporters joined a protest by the extremist Earth First! group at the Allegheny National Forest office in Warren, which resulted in protestors taking over the building and fastening themselves together with steel tubes and a bicycle lock.[18] ADP since has continued its association with Earth First! by receiving funding from the Fund for Wild Nature, the outlaw environmental faction's grant-making arm.[19]

Pursuing its goal to end commercial logging on the Allegheny, ADP – fueled by the Sierra Club and its campaign to halt logging on all National Forests – attacks the Forest Service through legal channels too. Beginning with a 1997 suit to stop the "Mortality II" logging project and continuing through a 2005 appeal, ADP has dragged the USFS staff into court nearly continuously for the better part of a decade.

However, in 2001, as ADP announced a lawsuit against the Allegheny's East Side logging project, an unexpected ally emerged on the Forest Service's behalf. "We had for years followed forest management projects through until they got litigated and then we were done," says Mark Banker, Regional Biologist for the Ruffed Grouse Society. "But we started to feel that there was a scientific perspective we could bring in the courtroom that wasn't there previously."

With Banker as the point man, RGS became an intervenor on behalf of the Allegheny National Forest in the 2001 lawsuit filed by ADP, the Sierra Club, and others. It was the first time since its 1961 inception that RGS involved itself in such a suit.

Banker believes in shining the harsh light of empirical evidence on the largely emotional and aesthetic arguments for putting an end to logging on National Forests. "People think you should have old forests and old growth everywhere," Banker says, his voice rising, "but there is a real and serious decline in early successional forest nearly everywhere in the East. And a lot of that is because the prevailing attitude is keeping the Forest Service from cutting trees when they need to."

With Banker presenting evidence that young forests – so critical to ruffed grouse, woodcock, and non-game species such as the yellow-breasted chat, eastern towhee, and field sparrow – is on the decline and that commercial timber cutting can be part of an ecologically sound approach to forestry, the US Third District Court ruled in 2004 in favor of the USFS on nine of ten counts in the East Side Project decision (ADP has since appealed).

"Based on the success of the East Side Project," Banker says today, "RGS became involved in the Bark Camp [Project] lawsuit on the Jefferson National Forest [Virginia], a state lawsuit in Michigan, and more recently on a group of National Forests in the Lake States, where the Sierra Club wanted to stop aspen management."

So far, his application of science in court has a perfect record. The USFS, with RGS support, won the East Side and Bark Camp suits. And though the other two suits never made it to court, "We came out ahead," says Banker.

Banker's zeal doesn't only cover science and ruffed grouse. He also believes fervently that when pursuing grouse, there is only one acceptable flavor of bird dog – one with a silky white coat and a long, feathered tail.

On that point, Banker and I have come to something of an accord – or at least set up a demilitarized zone. The bounds are thus: I tolerate his wing-footed, flitting English Setters as they find and point birds across a two time zone radius, and

I pretend not to be offended when he refers to Hunter as "Bullwinkle." Banker, on the other hand, has learned to remain vigilant so my gray locomotive doesn't take out his knees when we're navigating thick brush. Also, I suspect he's come to admire Hunter's retrieving skills.

Banker and I met in early November for a day of woodcock and grouse hunting on the Allegheny. Our first stop was Little Drummer, an ecological and historical interpretive area created through the cooperative efforts of RGS and USFS. Little Drummer shows a fascinating cross-section of the Allegheny as a "Land of Many Uses." Stops along an interpretive trail highlight abandoned logging railroads, bluebird boxes, an historic gas pipeline, and an aspen regeneration project. Since it was woodcock and grouse we were after, the aspen cuts were considerably more interesting than the gas pipeline, historic or not.

As we unloaded the dogs, Banker mentioned that RGS had done a lot of work on the Allegheny over the years, but on-the-ground projects have stopped recently due to the lawsuits and resultant moratorium on active management. Though happy about the East Side victory, Banker told me another lawsuit was already in the works over the Allegheny's Martin Run salvage cut and I could tell that the tedious and time-consuming effort of dealing with the battles was stressful.

"We're really anxious to start working up here on the Allegheny again," he said as we walked into the woods. "The lawsuits make it tough though."

We moved north through a stand of mature spruce and hemlock with Hunter and Banker's setter Bode gliding below the branches in front of us. Well, frankly, Bode glides; Hunter, who outweighs the setter by about 50 pounds, chugs.

Preferences for coat color and tail length aside, I have to admit that if I've ever seen a dog as good at finding and pointing birds as Bode, I can't remember it. The little setter is simply a joy to watch – at least when I could keep track of him. Accustomed to Hunter's more leisurely pace, I was amazed to see that fluff of white tail disappear from one spot and reappear a split second later impossibly far away. Speedy and silent, Bode drifted through even the thickest brush like a wisp of fog on a morning breeze.

We moved from the evergreens into a marshy area with low stands of patchy brush. Banker announced, "Point," and gestured toward a quivering Bode. Before we could walk in, the grouse flushed and flew behind us. We both whirled 180 degrees to follow the bird, but with Banker in my field of fire I had no shot. He managed to crack off one chamber, but it was a miss and the bird disappeared into the evergreens we had just walked through.

We reversed field and followed. We hadn't gone 100 yards into the shady forest when Hunter disappeared under a low-hanging hemlock. Mistakenly thinking he had continued out the other side, I walked a few steps past the tree then heard the grouse thunder up behind me – back in the direction it had flown in from.

I hollered for Banker and we once again doubled back on our steps. This time, though, the bird had gotten the better of us and we weren't able to catch up to it again.

As we marched, we passed through a mix of young forest habitat: oak saplings growing up around downed logs, mixed alder and dogwood stands, striped maple with black birch, and a few thick stands of aspen. There were no more birds in this stand, but Banker was impressed with the quality of the habitat.

"I figured that a lot of this would be overmature for grouse by now," he said, "but there's some really nice, thick stuff in here. Pausing for a moment, he added almost wistfully, "I'd still like to get our new tree shear up here and get at some of the older stuff."

We eventually came out to the interpretive path and decided to walk downhill parallel to it. This took us through even more brushy habitat. About halfway down the grade, Hunter started getting excited, but unfortunately it wasn't a bird he was after. Instead, he had found the single beast that birddog owners on the Allegheny fear above all others: the porcupine.

As Hunter hurtled around a flat rock the size of a kitchen table, I caught a glimpse of a quilly tail disappearing beyond it. My shouted "Whoa!" didn't stop the dog entirely, but luckily it slowed him enough to let the porky slide into a cranny under the rock. I could still see the quills on the tail - as sharp and deadly looking as sabers to my eyes - poking out from under the rock, but I managed to get Hunter collared and led away before he could get his mouth around the dangerous critter.

With that bit of misadventure behind us, we cruised to a beaver pond, its margins marshy and thick with alder and dogwood. One look at this habitat and we both had woodcock on the brain.

In the interest of covering more ground, Banker suggested that we split up and meet again at the back edge of the pond. I agreed, so he and Bode went off to the left while Hunter and I went around the right.

Within five minutes, I regretted the decision as I heard two quick shots from Banker's Beretta 686 20 gauge. When I heard another shot from the over and under, followed by two more a few minutes later, it didn't cheer me up any.

By the time we met at the back of the pond, Bode and Banker had flushed five different birds, all grouse. Hunter and I hadn't found a single bird.

"So how many did you get?" I asked.

"Um," he replied, looking down at the dog, "None. I'm just shooting terrible." At least that cheered me up a little bit.

"Come on," he said. "I want to take you back around here and see if we can get a couple of those birds up again. Maybe we'll have a better chance to kill one."

"Taking me along is not exactly a cure for bad shooting," I reminded him.

"That's true," Banker agreed, "but two guns are still going to be better than one. Twice as much lead in the air, twice the chances of getting a bird."

We gradually worked our way back around the pond. Not finding any of the birds Banker flushed, we veered off toward the west into an area we hadn't covered yet. As we watched the dogs work ahead of us, we talked some more about logging controversies on the Allegheny.

Despite all the rhetoric about sustainable forestry, old growth, and tree hugging, the timber debates on the Allegheny, in a sense, come down to just one species – black cherry. For a variety of geographical, geological, and ecological reasons, the finest black cherry timber in the world is grown in northern Pennsylvania, much of it within the Allegheny National Forest. As a Pennsylvania lumberman once told me, "If you buy a piece of cherry furniture anywhere in the United States or in about half the other countries in the world, chances are it came from here."

Dr. Stout backs up this claim. "The cherry range is huge. It reaches from New England to Texas and most areas in between. There are even cherries in Chile. But," she concluded, "this [location] really is the best."

The commercial value of the Allegheny's black cherry has created an unusual set of circumstances for this National Forest. For one, the desire to cut timber on the Allegheny nearly always remains high; it consistently ranks near the top in value of wood products sold in USFS's Eastern Region. Further, the Allegheny is one of a small fraction of National Forests on which commercial logging is a profitable venture. As Stout notes, "It's physically a very small Forest, but due to the cherry the economic return is competitive with much larger forests."

This profitability has led to charges that the Allegheny is being managed as one giant black cherry farm. ADP's Talbott says, "The Forest Service doesn't want to do anything that interferes with their black cherry crop. They say that they're not managing for black cherry, but when I go out to these timber sales and I see what they're doing – the areas they're selecting to cut, the application of herbicides – I just don't see it. Everything's geared toward growing black cherry."

Stout, naturally, is quick to dispute that claim. "Our science suggests that a whole variety of factors outside of management choices are pushing [forest] regeneration toward cherry," she says. Specifically, she lists resistance to acid rain, prolific production and spreading of seeds, and the fact that black cherry is one of the last tree species that white-tailed deer will eat.

Many zero-cut proponents like ADP and the Sierra Club claim that the Allegheny is becoming a monoculture of black cherry, but in more than six months scouting and hunting across the entire Forest, I didn't see so much as a single stand consisting of just cherry, mature or immature. However, there are spots like one that Banker and I found at Little Drummer, where that species is by far the dominant tree.

This particular location was a mix of mature cherries, hemlocks, and oaks. Compared to the thick stands we had just left, these woods were very much open and frankly didn't look much like ruffed grouse habitat. Apparently someone forgot to tell the birds that though.

As we entered a small clearing bounded by tall hemlocks, a grouse flushed wild in front of Banker, on my left. I never saw the bird and wasn't even sure I had heard it until he fired. Although that shot missed, it prompted a second bird to flush from the same spot. This time, feet already set and gun at his shoulder, Banker didn't miss.

Bode moved to retrieve the downed bird, but at the last minute he had a change of heart and moved on to look for the one that escaped. Banker started the long walk over to pick up the downed grouse.

At about this moment I noticed Hunter standing in front of me. He had been off to my right when the shooting started and had come out of the trees at the sound of Banker's shot. Sorting out the commotion, he seemed to realize that it hadn't been me shooting. Then he looked up and saw Banker moving toward the fluttering bird. This was apparently more than the gray dog was willing to tolerate.

Bounding across the clearing like a runaway train, Hunter beat Banker to the downed grouse by less than a step. Just as the biologist was starting to bend, the dog shouldered past with body language that seemed to say, "I hope you don't think *you're* going to pick up this bird."

Then, lifting the bird into his jaws, he brushed by Banker again and trotted toward me, head held high. Fairly prancing across the little meadow, Hunter proudly delivered Banker's grouse into my waiting hands.

That, I shouldn't have to tell you, cheered me up immensely.

By the time we got back to the trucks it was just after 11 AM. Banker had to leave by mid-afternoon so we decided to head off to another spot and maximize the time in the field rather than running back to Ridgway for lunch.

We decided to head just a few miles up the road to another RGS project known as Owls Nest. This spot has a remarkable history not only as a major habitat project, but also as the location of one of the most destructive forest fires in the history of Pennsylvania, and perhaps the eastern US.

The conditions that allowed the Bear Creek fire to blaze onto the pages of history began in the early 1900s when the US Leather Company was formed. This massive conglomerate, the tenth largest business in the country at the time, was trying to consolidate all of the tanning hemlock across northern Pennsylvania. Through their subsidiary, the Central Pennsylvania Lumber Company, US Leather operated 20 saw mills across the region, with the largest located in Sheffield, in the heart of what is now the Allegheny National Forest.

According to author Mike Schultz, "[I]n 1920, the company turned its attention to a 20,000-acre plot in Bear Creek, Elk County, the largest remaining hemlock forest east of the Mississippi." By the time the Bear Creek cut was finished in 1926, "[n]early 15,000 acres of logging slash filled the area [and a]nother 10,000 acres of stripped land lay adjacent..."[20]

With low rainfalls in 1925 and a dry spring in 1926, a brutal and deadly catastrophe crept closer on each breath of wind.

The fire (actually three simultaneous fires) broke out on May 17, 1926, perhaps from a USFS crew that had been burning brush the day before. By the second day, nearly 30,000 acres were in flames. Owls Nest, "a tiny gas-lease settlement of less than ten homes," was hemmed in by a wall of fire that stormed in from the north.[21] Making a brave stand against the thunderous inferno, firefighters were able to stave off the flames immediately around the homes and most of the village was saved. From there the fire jumped past them and swept east.

Among the daring exploits of the firefighters and civilians battling the blaze, Schultz tells the following: "A lease worker drove his truck at breakneck speed toward Owls Nest as he barely escaped the fire's wrath. Within minutes after he had arrived, the fire hit the hamlet. As he rushed to put out the exploding fires, he yelled, "Ain't this a helluva note. I ran from one fire straight into another one."[22]

Finally, on May 19, a welcome rainstorm hit and the nearly 1,000 firefighters were able to wrest it under control. During the three hellish days, at least two people were killed and CPL lost over 10 million board feet of logs, along with miles of railroad line and bridges.

Decades later, as the woods near Owls Nest eventually matured, USFS and RGS partnered to once again cut them back. This time, instead of hemlock bark for leather tanning, the goal was habitat regeneration for early successional wildlife. The young forest that resulted is almost inconceivably thick in places and made up of a dense weave of black birch, maple, and oak – an excellent lurking place for ruffed grouse.

Banker and I pulled up to a gated Forest Service road and parked across from the sign that advertised the cooperative demonstration project of RGS and USFS. Giving Bode a much-deserved break, Banker let his younger dog, Suzie, out for the first time today.

As we walked south through the occasionally impenetrable thickets, Banker and I quickly lost sight of each other and could only keep tabs by sporadically calling out. As we entered one especially thick patch, a rabbit burst out in front of Hunter and leapt past me, barely avoiding the tips of my boots.

I automatically swung the gun to my left and gave what amounted to a parting blast as the bunny disappeared. As the shrapnel from the wounded saplings and briars settled, I turned to see Banker staring at me.

I suddenly worried that I had committed a major *faux pas*, perhaps *the* major *faux pas* to a grouse hunter: I had actually taken a shot at something running along the ground, something with fur rather than feathers. For a fleeting second, I thought the offense might cause Banker to pick up his dog and stalk out, or worse, simply keel over from an aneurysm.

He's probably heavier than he looks, I thought, and how would I explain it to his wife if I just left him here?

I wonder if she would let me keep Bode?

As it turned out, Banker neither left nor croaked. In fact, he told me later that he wasn't above taking the occasional potshot at a rabbit either. Guess I would have to find another way to adopt Bode.

We followed the gentle drift of a broad hollow downhill. As the ground flattened out at the bottom of the draw, we found ourselves in gorgeous grouse and woodcock habitat: young aspens giving way to a swampy red maple/dogwood/alder bottom. Unfortunately we discovered that no one had told the birds about this beautiful stand; we had nary a flush.

At this point, we were probably two miles from the parking spot and a problem presented itself. Hunter's pads were bleeding from what my vet later diagnosed as an allergic reaction. Although he had been admirably keeping pace with Suzie since we arrived at Owls Nest, he now started limping badly. Having seen Hunter ignore torn pads and various thorn injuries in the past, I was a little surprised that he would go lame in the field, but after watching him hobble it was clearly time to call it a day.

We turned back uphill, taking a more direct route to the trucks. This took us through more spectacular grouse habitat, thick pines around the edges of regenerating clearcuts. When we crested the hill, Banker turned to me suddenly and said, "I'm sold. This is all tremendous habitat."

As we approached the trucks, we bumped into two bow hunters who were just going into the woods to set up for an evening whitetail hunt. After a quick round of small talk, they told us they had just flushed three grouse from the edge of the trail, not 30 yards from where we stood. As the pair moved off deeper into the woods, Banker and I decided to take Suzie on one quick swing through the brush to see if we could roust the birds, but it was a futile effort. They were long gone.

Back at the vehicles, we sat down to rest our legs for a moment and I took advantage of the opportunity to get a closer look at Hunter's feet. This inspection showed bleeding pads in several spots, but I also caught a glimpse of something alongside one of the nails on his back paw. Thinking it was a thorn, I grabbed a pair of needle-nosed pliers and, ignoring Hunter's complaints, latched on to the offending article. After a few seconds of wrestling, I extracted a two-inch porcupine quill that had been jammed in so far into his toe that only about a quarter-inch was left exposed.

Banker winced when I held up the quill for inspection. "Oh, man!" he groaned. "He's probably had that thing in there since we saw that porky this morning!"

"Yep," I nodded as the gray snout smeared grateful slobber all over my face.

"Can you imagine?" asked Banker. "He walked all day with that thing stuck in there. I couldn't have gone more than about 10 feet like that."

"Yeah, me neither," I replied. I gently scrubbed Hunter's droopy ears, trying to stash away my guilt for not having found the quill when I first checked him. "He's tougher than he looks."

Banker started to pick the burrs from Suzie's coat. Both of us were reluctant to let this golden day end, so we plopped on the bank and, with a furry head and floppy ears tucked comfortably in each of our laps, chatted a little longer.

As far as Banker is concerned, the Allegheny "ranks pretty high" as a grouse hunting destination, at least among National Forests in the Eastern Region. "It certainly ranks higher than most any place south of Pennsylvania," he said. But he feels that the Allegheny isn't nearly as good as it could be for young forest species. "The last 10, 15 years, the ANF has lost a lot of value for grouse and woodcock hunting [due to less cutting]. My sense is that things may be cranking back up, but it's definitely not as good as it was in the 80s."

He stressed that RGS doesn't support logging every inch of the National Forest. "We don't oppose Wilderness designation for appropriate areas. We *do* oppose taking lands that don't have a wilderness character today out of the management base when so little [logging] is being done already. There are all sorts of *de facto* Wilderness areas on the Allegheny. Probably 30, 40 percent of that Forest is going to be designated unsuitable for timbering [in the new Forest Plan]."

The point that seems to gall Banker most is that the concept of eliminating commercial logging is based largely on emotional ideals, rather than empirical data. Indeed, much of the rhetoric from anti-logging factions is laced with near hysterical language like "destructive network of clearcuts"[23] and "ravaged wasteland"[24]

In discussing a zero-cut policy, Banker is blunt: "It's just not supported by any science that we're aware of. It just makes no sense."

Clearly, it makes perfect sense to groups like ADP and the Sierra Club. In 2002, the Sierra Club released a letter signed by over 200 scientists from across the nation urging President Bush to "end the destructive practice of commercial logging in the National Forests..."

Meanwhile other academics, like Penn State Professor of Forest Resources Jim Finley, defend the Forest Service's sustainable forestry policies. "Those who say that we should allow forests to manage themselves," says Finley, "are not considering the extent of problems that past human decisions and activities have already imposed. We need many of the resources the forests create and provide, and we have to provide the best resources we can to future generations. The Allegheny National Forest is a crown jewel of the United States Forest Service's National Forest System and has an excellent record of careful science-based forest management."[25]

When sifting through the claims of both sides, the charges and countercharges, the science and counterscience, it's virtually impossible to get a clear answer. As one of the judges in the East Side lawsuit said, the case was "absolutely the most complex I have ever dealt with."[26]

However, a few months spent on the Allegheny – truly looking at the woods and the life within them – can provide the kind of insight not found in a courtroom. Seeing the dense biomass and the diverse productivity of regenerating clearcuts, feeling the sting of saplings whipping your ears, hearing the wingbeats against still air as a grouse bursts from thick brush and churns skyward, you can sense for yourself that cutting timber on the Allegheny is not ruining the Forest. It's renewing it.

What's more, your time doesn't have to be spent just in the impenetrable grouse and woodcock covers to get a sense that the woods will be rejuvenated. The majestic stands of mature trees that forest preservation advocates are so passionate about form their own tangible evidence. These mature stands have regrown from clearcutting and forest fires far more devastating than anything allowed under modern environmental controls. There's no evidence to suggest that active and selective management can't keep the Allegheny producing black cherry timber, a variety of forest habitats, clean water, and quality hunting opportunities for many decades to come.

When I spoke to ADP's Talbott, he said, "Values do come into the equation. You have to say, Is this an appropriate way to handle a public resource?"

From my view of the Allegheny, the answer to that question is a definitive "Yes."

CHAPTER 7

TALKING TURKEY

Maybe it was due to my lack of success in earlier seasons or maybe it was because Thanksgiving was just around the bend, but the night before my ANF turkey hunt, I dreamed of the big, black, bearded birds all night long.

Truth be told, the reason for my gobbling night visitors was most likely the tales that Dan Brophy had spun for me the day before. The younger brother of my longtime coworker and softball teammate Ed Brophy, Dan had enthusiastically agreed to guide me on an Allegheny National Forest turkey hunt. Then he primed the pump.

As he told it, Dan, an avid waterfowler, had a tough decision to make as November arrived. "I wanted to hunt turkeys, but ducks were also coming in," he told me, "and so was bow season [for deer]. I wanted to hunt for all of them, so I decided to go after turkeys first since that would be the easiest one of the three."

It's no accident that turkey hunting on the Allegheny has improved to the point that hanging a tag on a fall bird is one of the surer bets in the woods. The improvement in turkey populations is the result of a concentrated effort in habitat restoration for nearly the past two decades, led primarily by the National Wild Turkey Federation.

Since 1988, NWTF has spent over a quarter-million dollars on the Allegheny National Forest, creating about 3,355 acres of new and improved turkey habitat. Projects have ranged from planting a few apple trees to the 1000-acre Bear Creek/Clarion River project, which, at the time of its initiation, was the largest habitat project ever undertaken by NWTF.[27]

The close relationship between the USFS and NWTF on the Allegheny is more the rule than the exception for National Forests. In fact, the relationship between the two groups is so cozy that the Forest Service has arranged for employee Dennis Daniel to set up housekeeping in NWTF's national office in Edgefield, South Carolina.

Daniel, the National Coordinator for the Forest Service with NWTF, explains that, "Legislation allowed the Forest Service to receive money from outside agencies and at the same time, NWTF wanted a place on public land to spend dollars." It was a natural fit so that, "The common guy who has to hunt on public land can see the benefits."

According to Daniel, NWTF has spent about $4.5 million on National Forests since the 1986 agreement was signed. "They've done projects in every [USFS] region except 10, which is Alaska," he says proudly.

Some of the highlight projects include ongoing efforts to restore the Gould's turkey in Arizona's Coronado National Forest, as well as habitat improvements like prescribed fires and riparian restorations in other states. The relationship has sunk its roots deep over the years, with many USFS employees getting involved in NWTF, even starting their own chapters. "They're out there building relationships and working on the ground," says Daniel, "it's been invaluable to both the Forest Service and NWTF."

He wasn't the only one that was bullish on National Forest turkey populations. Back on the Allegheny, Dan Brophy was "hell-bent on getting one, especially because [turkey hunting] is so good up here."

Because he's currently a student and a Pennsylvania National Guard reservist, Dan has the luxury of free time, so he decided to put it to use in the woods. He went to his family's camp along the Allegheny River on the first Tuesday of the season. Getting out during the week is one of the great secrets of Allegheny National Forest hunting. As Dan said, "I had the whole woods to myself."

Having heavily scouted birds on the mountain west of camp, Dan knew that they would fly directly from their hemlock roosts to the privacy of Baker Island, part of the federally-designated Allegheny River Islands Wilderness. Because the frigid November waters keep most hunters away, the birds have the place more or less to themselves and they rarely vary their routine. Dan wasn't intending to change that pattern so he slept in and spent the morning running errands, taking care of some chores around Camp Brophy, and doing a little grouse and squirrel hunting.

Around lunchtime, just as he crested the ridge of a mountain near camp, the skies opened and, for the ten-thousandth day in a row, it poured rain. Undaunted, Dan worked his way across the top of the mountain then slipped quietly among the raindrops down a hollow where he knew turkeys sometimes fed. There were none home today, however, and Dan, soaked and hungry, decided to go downhill to camp, the promise of lunch, and some warm, dry clothes.

Once back in the comfort of camp, he let his black Lab Cassie out of her crate for a romp once the downpour let up. Then, stripped to his boxers, he tossed a couple of hot dogs in a skillet and wandered out in the yard to enjoy a few minutes of lack of rain.

"I couldn't believe it!" Dan ranted to me later. "A whole freakin' flock of turkeys flew across from the island, just downriver. They were within 100 yards of camp!"

Mostly naked, Dan went into full panic mode. "I threw my clothes back on and shoved Cassie in her crate," he chuckled. Then he ran down the road to see if he could find the spot where the flock marched up the mountain. Unfortunately, he couldn't find so much as a track or a dropped feather so he gave up and headed back to camp once again.

As soon as he stepped back through the door, Dan realized he had spent more time than intended chasing after the ghost turkeys. His plan for the afternoon had been to set up on the western ridge then wait for the birds to fly back from the island and intercept them on their way to the roost. To accomplish that he would need to be sitting well up the ridge well before dark. Now it was just an hour and a half until sunset and he was still in camp, choking down the remains of the hot dogs he had cooked two hours ago.

Unwilling to give up, Dan finally switched to dry clothes and jumped in his truck. He drove a half-mile north toward the town of West Hickory then pulled the over to the berm. "As soon as I closed the door," he told me, "it started to drizzle again."

With the cooler evening temperatures, a thick fog also rolled in off the river and crept its way up the ridge. "You could barely see 50 yards," he recalled.

Anxious to make up time, Dan sprinted up the steep hillside through the mist. Finding his spot, he swept into place, yanking his facemask down and pulling on his gloves in one motion. "I was still catching my breath," he recounted, "and here come these turkeys out of the fog. It was cool because it seemed like they just appeared out of the air." Sweating and winded, he had an even harder time catching his breath when he realized that the five birds materializing out of the damp evening air were all gobblers, each with long, swaying beards.

The flock of toms slowly picked their way up the hillside toward Dan, stopping to peck and eat as they marched.

When the group closed to 15 yards, they turned and walked crossways in front of the hidden hunter. "I wanted to shoot one then," Dan said, "but I decided that I wanted to watch them even more. So I just kept waiting and watching them."

Suddenly, the gobblers stopped as one and began to look around. Fearing that they were getting nervous and might bolt before he got a shot, Dan shifted the Mossberg 835 slightly to put the fattest tom in his sights.

When he pulled the trigger, "that bird dropped like a ton of bricks."

When he got the big bird back to camp, he found that it had an eight-inch beard, one inch spurs, and weighed a solid 19 ½ pounds. As he reflected on the afternoon, Dan realized that he had spent more time watching the flock of five than it had taken him to get up the hill and get set up. "The fog is what helped," he observed. "That and the rain all day. There were no leaves crunching when I ran up the hill."

Despite the wet morning, the disappearing birds at lunch, and the hurried start to the evening, "it worked out perfectly," he concluded.

Thrilling as it sounded, that wasn't the only story Dan told me that contributed to my gobbler dreams. He also mentioned that four days later his father, Ed Sr., shot another tom just a few dozen yards from the spot Dan shot his. On top of that, a group of Dan's buddies shot two more birds the following week, just two days before our phone conversation.

"Don't worry, though," he assured me, "There are 30 or 40 in this flock and they haven't changed their pattern at all, even with the hunting pressure." He mentioned that he was still seeing the flock fly back and forth to the island while he was duck hunting.

"Come on up and we'll definitely get you a shot at a turkey," he ended confidently.

What could I say? He had me at "Hello." That, and "eight inch beard."

I arranged to meet Dan around 1 PM on a Friday, and from there we would use the same strategy he had employed to get his bird – intercepting them on their way back from Baker Island to their roost. When I pulled into Camp Brophy, I met Dan in person for the first time, but we didn't have time to waste on pleasantries so we were quickly in his truck and down the dirt road. Dan mentioned several times that "this little bit of rain is perfect since it will keep those birds in their pattern."

Within a half-hour, we were snuggling our backs against the root mass of a cherry tree blowdown. From that spot we had a clear view down the ridge for perhaps 75 yards.

As we settled in and waited for the birds to make their nightly assault on the ridge, Dan and I finally had a chance to share a whispered conversation. He mentioned that he was studying environmental science at nearby Slippery Rock University and that he was expecting to graduate in the spring.

"Did your brother tell you that I manage our environmental department at work?" I asked.

"He just told me that this past week," he whispered back.

"You should send me a resume when you're ready to start looking," I told him.

"Sure," he replied eagerly. "Working at the same company with Ed would be cool."

"Well," I sniffed, "we'll see if I get a bird this afternoon. Then I'll tell you if it's cool or not." Dan stifled a snicker.

The next three hours passed with nary a bird. Dan seemed crushed. A half-dozen times he repeated, "I was so sure that the birds would come in here to roost." I guiltily tried to boost his spirits, assuring him that the literal and figurative black cloud that had been following me around this season wasn't his fault, but it didn't seem to console him much.

What finally did help was a couple of hours spent leaning on the red-and-white checkered tablecloth that adorns the worn kitchen table back at Camp Brophy. We had two hours before Dan's wife, Sara – who, God bless her, is not only the wife of a soldier and avid hunter, but also mom to an active toddler named Ryder – and his parents, Ed Sr. and Char, would arrive. So in true hunting camp fashion we killed the time by tossing our caps on the table, tilting our chairs back, and swapping our best tales, savoring the delicious rhythm of one punch line followed by another.

Describing the photos mounted on the kitchen wall one by one, Dan relayed to me the history of the camp since his dad bought it in 1990. Just 11 at the time, Dan had essentially grown up hunting and fishing here. We talked about past bucks and big bass, goose hunts, and the banded wood duck that Dan shot on the Allegheny River last year. For the most part, the conversation revolved around Dan's passion for duck hunting and for the Allegheny National Forest.

Eventually the conversation turned to his enlistment in the National Guard. "After 9/11," he said slowly, groping for the right words, "I just...I just felt like I had to do it." He was staring over my shoulder, uncomfortably avoiding my gaze.

Seeking to share something that I could never really be a part of, I told Dan that I had also looked into volunteering for the service after the September 11 attacks.

"Unfortunately," I grinned, trying to an awkward and heavy moment, "they wouldn't take me because I was already an old fart...at 36 years old!" He cracked a grin and the self-conscious instant passed.

Shortly, the phone started ringing and after a coordination effort that Dan's commanding officer would have envied, it was finally determined that we would meet the family a couple of miles upriver at their usual Friday night gathering spot, the Hickory Nut Inn. When we got there, Sara and Ryder were already waiting in the parking lot, and Ed, Sr. and Char arrived about 20 minutes later.

After Dan introduced me, we three guys quickly gravitated to one end of the table and the hunting talk resumed. We recounted our lack of success on turkeys that afternoon. Ed shared Dan's surprise that we hadn't seen any birds, and then told the story of the bird he had shot two weeks before. When I first heard this tale from Dan earlier in the week, it sounded encouraging. Now, after a wet, fruitless afternoon in the woods it felt more like lemon juice in a paper cut. Ed and Dan reminded me, however, that we still had tomorrow. They were both sure we'd get our crack then.

Over greasy plates of Cajun wings and French fries, all washed down by Iron City beer –which the waitress delivered to Ed without being asked, the very definition of being a regular – we spun as many hunting yarns as could be repeated in mixed company. I was excited to find out that Ed had hunted on the Allegheny National Forest for more than three decades and he indulged my interest with stories of how hunting on the Allegheny used to be.

We heard about years when the meat pole at camp bent low, years of bitter cold and deep snows, and, of course, about big bucks. As Ed and Dan pointed out though, the definition of a big buck on the Allegheny – at least since the 1960s – is an 8-point. Rarely do they get much bigger due to herd size, habitat condition, and, most of all, intense hunting pressure.

This discussion led in turn to talk of deer management and the recent implementation of antler restrictions across Pennsylvania. In Wildlife Management Unit 2F, which includes the Allegheny, buck harvest is restricted to those with at least three points on one side. Since I'm a strong proponent of reining in deer numbers and trying to let the habitat reestablish, I naturally back this effort.

Ed, Sr., on the other hand, was raised in the "see 'em, shoot 'em" school of whitetail hunting and isn't interested in changing now. This places him squarely among the vocal many hunters who feel that antler restrictions and increases in antlerless tags are going to permanently ruin deer hunting in the Keystone State.

While the combination of a philosophical disagreement and multiple pitchers of beer would have normally made for a crisp give and take, I suddenly remembered that Ed owned the camp I was hoping to sleep in tonight...and that it was pretty chilly outside. With that realization, I found myself nodding my head a lot as he spoke.

Eventually the conversation swung back to the plan of attack for tomorrow. From Dan's descriptions of duck hunting on the river, I was itching to give that a try. But I also knew tomorrow was the last day of fall turkey season, and I hated to pass up that chance. I was hesitating over this point when Dan floated a solution.

"Well," he started slowly, "the turkey hunting really is better in the afternoon since the birds fly over to the island in the morning. We could hunt ducks in the morning then still have plenty of time to hunt turkeys in the afternoon."

I rose to the bait and slammed it like one of the bass on the Camp Brophy brag board. "That sounds great!" I chirped and when Ed agreed to tag along on the morning duck hunt and the itinerary was set.

I had no clue what the ladies had been discussing for the past hour or so, but whatever it was, it had run its course and they were now staring at us expectantly. With tomorrow's schedule now set, we were out of excuses to order another pitcher of Iron, so we settled the tab and closed up shop. We were back at camp and in bed by 11:30.

By the time Dan and I rolled out of our rooms at 5:30 the next morning, Ed was already working on egg sandwiches for breakfast. It didn't even take a glance out the window to know that it was raining yet again.

After breakfast, the three of us and Cassie the Lab piled into my pickup for the short drive downriver. When the road petered out, we parked and walked another half-mile or so further in the inky pre-dawn. At that point, we turned left, skidded down the steep bank to the river, and waded across a hip-deep backwater to the southern tip of an unnamed island.

Dan and I set a cluster of mallard and wood duck decoys in the still water of the back channel then the three of us clambered into the limbs of a downed tree at the southern tip of the island. We crouched where each of us could watch a different direction and settled in to wait for first light.

As the sun crept over the east rim of the valley, a blue heron glided upriver over our decoy spread. From my vantage point, I saw it swoop up into a snag and settle on a branch overhanging the backwater. A few minutes later a pair of belted kingfishers sailed overhead, but it was a half-hour past sunup and there was not a duck or goose to be seen. While my continuing bad hunting luck this fall had already conditioned me this type of thing, the Brophys were almost comical in their puzzlement over the lack of birds.

Shortly, the answer to the absence of ducks reached our ears as power boats began to scream upriver. We quickly surmised that a smallmouth tournament was scheduled on the river that morning and we had unwittingly set our decoy spread virtually in the middle of it. Climbing to a higher vantage point, we could see at least four boats bobbing in the water near the mouth of Tionesta Creek and two more running upriver at high speed.

Dan was livid at the presence of the boats and the absence of ducks. "I didn't know the Tionesta Regatta was going to be this weekend," he griped in disgust.

In a last ditch effort, the three of us marched up to the northern end of the island in hopes of jump shooting a duck or two from one of the inlets along its edge. When that effort also struck out, we packed up the decoys and hiked back to the truck.

After switching to drier clothes back at camp and helping Ed pack away some camp equipment for the winter, Dan and I determined our best bet would be an amphibious assault on the turkey stronghold at Baker Island. Dan, always vigilant on the regulations, suggested that we should wear the required blaze orange but load our guns with steel shot on the chance that we might jump some ducks.

Thus, oddly dressed for duck hunting and oddly loaded for turkeys, we drove upriver and slipped the Brophy's aluminum Grumman canoe into the frigid gray water. I have to admit, as we paddled downstream and the canoe pitched on the rough, bitingly cold waves, I questioned the wisdom of this maneuver.

We pulled up on a gravel bar on the north end of Baker Island and dragged the canoe out. We figured to walk the island from north to south in an attempt to scatter a flock of turkeys without sending them off across the river. If we could manage that trick, we felt we could call them back in fairly easily.

Baker Island's habitat, mature cottonwoods and maples interspersed with large brushy fields of goldenrod and willows, was carved every few feet with muddied deer trails and we found turkey droppings atop several downed logs. Leaves were scattered where the birds had been scratching for food, but, the only game we saw was a pair of does we kicked out near the edge of a small inlet. Once again, there were no birds to be found.

Dan and I looped back to the canoe and nosed it into the water. As we drifted downstream to investigate the islands near camp, a flock of a dozen ducks zipped upriver toward us.

It was at least a 40-yard shot, but there was ammo in the gun and no reason to hold back, so Dan and I each cracked off a shot as they blew by. Naturally, we both missed cleanly.

We turned to watch the birds as they disappeared upriver but before I turned back, Dan looked over my shoulder and yelled, "Here comes another bunch!" I spun just in time to see a flock of five buffleheads winging nearly overhead. I had only one shot left in the old Crescent and it punched a hole in the misty air a good four feet behind the last duck. Dan was so flustered – either at the sudden appearance of two flocks of ducks or at my incredibly poor shooting, I'm not sure which – that he didn't even get off a shot.

Sodden and disgusted, we drifted in silence. As we neared camp, we paddled to the far side of yet another island and snuck the canoe quietly around its southern tip. We hoped to jump the ducks that Dan sometimes finds loafing there, but there were none to be jumped today.

Not quite willing to accept defeat on the water yet, we pulled the canoe up onto the next island and walked it looking for either ducks or turkeys. We went no more than a dozen steps when a large flock of geese honked their way upriver, much too far out for a shot. Dan figured that they probably wanted to land on the gravel bar next to this island, and as if to prove his point, the birds circled anxiously over us not once but twice. Unfortunately, in our safety orange hats and vests we stood out like a pair of rhinos on a city street, and after the second pass the flock finally veered off for good.

Chins drooping, we paddled back upriver to Camp Brophy, stowed the canoe in the shed and slunk in through the kitchen door, glum and ready to surrender. It was then that, with a mother's unfailing sense of timing, Char swooped to the rescue with a savory lunch of fried kielbasa and onion sandwiches. We munched heartily and our hunting spirit returned, even as Ryder quizzed his dad over and over, "Ducks, Daddy? Ducks? Where the ducks?"

For the second time that day we changed into dry clothes and at about 3 PM we marched back out the door, hoping to close the last hours of fall turkey season with a bang. We strode quickly up the hillside, passing the spot we had set up the previous afternoon, and settling in back to back across a fallen log about 100 yards further uphill.

This too, though, was a wasted effort. Our sour luck held and we sat until dark without seeing or hearing a single turkey.

Dan was dejected. Desperate to make amends, he invited me back for the bear season opener on Monday. I told him that I was already committed to hunting at Camp Stockert.

"How about deer season then?" he offered helpfully, but I explained that I was locked in to hunting at Stockert's then too. Finally we settled on a waterfowl hunt later in the year, with the possibility of getting back together in May for spring gobblers as well.

I said my goodbyes at Camp Brophy and turned the F-150 south. I had a three-hour drive home, followed by an hour-and-a-half trip to my parent's tomorrow for an early Thanksgiving dinner. From there, I would head north again to Camp Stockert for the start of bear season.

It was nearly the end of November. Hopefully things would start heating up.

A Season on the Allegheny

PHOTOS

The remote Allegheny National Forest was one of the few locations in Pennsylvania where deer survived into the twentieth century

Hunter and the author calling geese at Buzzard Swamp

Dan Fitzgerald paddling on the Wild and Scenic Clarion River

Downed hemlocks on the Tionesta Research Natural Area

John Mack prowls the Beanfield in search of pheasants

Hunter retrieves a stolen grouse to the author

"*A whole freakin' flock of turkeys flew across from the island!*"

A PGC scientist examines a bruin at the Marienville Bear Check Station

*Camp Captain Ken Stockert shows off his deer,
a time-honored tradition*

Dan Brophy and Cassie pull a duck from the icy Allegheny River

Mary Hosmer (left) helps Nate Welker gear up for a snowshoe hare hunt

*The author's daughter, Rachel Hilliard,
looks to her future in the forest*

An old-fashioned gun and old-fashioned hunting at Tracy Ridge

"The essence of the chase changes little"

*A wildlife food plot on the Allegheny is
a fitting tribute to Len Kostelnik*

CHAPTER 8

OF BEARS AND BOYS

My father and stepmother would be traveling over Thanksgiving so my brood, along with those of my two younger sisters, was gathering at the ancestral home for a traditional turkey dinner on a nontraditional Sunday afternoon. The time was enjoyable and the meal was mouth-watering.

One holiday tradition to which my family firmly adheres is one that dates back to the earliest reaches of Thanksgiving in America - watching football. And so, as Rachel, Stephanie, and Jake played with their cousins in my dad's basement, Pam and I flopped in front of the warming glow of the big screen TV and watched the Steeler game with my parents, my sisters, and their husbands. Pittsburgh rolled the New York Giants to run their record to 13 - 1 as I hollered myself halfway hoarse. The spinach dip and crackers only soothed my throat a little.

Within minutes of the final gun we were slicing into a turkey baked to an autumnal shade of gold. I quickly dug myself a pile of mashed potatoes that was itself the size of a football and tried hard to keep from leaving even a crumb of stuffing for anyone else. Devouring the feast with my usual locust-like gusto, it seemed like only seconds before we were picking our favorites from my stepmom's selection of a dozen yummy desserts.

Sadly, though, I had to forgo my usual post-meal nap/coma in favor of climbing back in the cab of the silver pickup and driving north to the Allegheny National Forest and Camp Stockert. I sipped on a Mountain Dew as I pulled out of the driveway to make sure I didn't accidentally take that nap en route.

By the time I rolled up to camp and found a tiny gap to park between the crowd of trucks out front, it was well past 9 PM. But the late night and the scheduled early wakeup the next morning hadn't done much to diminish the enthusiasm within the walls of Camp Stockert.

There were a total of seven men in camp for the black bear hunt. Ken Stockert, the owner and "camp captain," is, like me, a biologist for a consulting firm in the Pittsburgh area. Stockert is a stocky, jovial man in his late 30s, with sandy, thinning hair and a habit of chuckling quietly at the end of his sentences. It's a tendency that makes everything he says sound warm and friendly – even when he's raking you over the coals, as is frequently the case.

Stockert and I had known each other for several years and talked hunting for most of them, but I never realized that he had a camp in the National Forest until I mentioned my book project to him. Although that conversation happened in mid-summer, it was only minutes before he was demanding my attendance at camp for a bear hunt.

Also joining us to chase bruins at Camp Stockert was Stockert's former brother-in-law, Jeff Novosel. That's correct, his *former* brother-in-law. Novosel was married for eight years to Stockert's older sister and, although Novosel wasn't a hunter when they met, he eventually became a regular during every season there. When the marriage ended, Novosel's association continued uninterrupted and he is now the elder statesman of Camp Stockert, proving that, though blood may be thicker than water, nobody is as thick as the guys at hunting camp.

The rest of the camp dwellers included Sean Riley, a longtime friend of Novosel's who had become a camp regular; Steve Paraska, another from Stockert's seemingly endless supply of brothers-in-law, this one from his wife Jodi's side of the family; and Jim and Mike Lacey, a father and son duo.

When I first stepped into camp, I could sense tension. That's because Stockert had, unbeknownst to me, prepped them with a few details of my book project, some background on my writing career, and a summary of our work together in our parallel careers. As a result, they were lying in wait like a pack of leopards watching a zebra walk under their tree. Only Paraska and the senior Lacey spared me, but that was only because they were already sound asleep in the back bunkroom.

"So," Riley challenged me before I even had a chance to pull up a chair at the table, "you're writing a book." It was more of a statement than a question.

"Yeah," I replied, shooting a sideways look at Stockert, who was grinning at me over a tall glass of Jim Beam and Coke.

"You're writing a book about hunting," Riley said. Another statement.

"Um, yeah," I answered again, still not sure where this series of declarations was going. Novosel, seated to my left, chuckled.

"It's about hunting?" This was an actual question from Mike.

"Yeah," I said, "Up here in the National Forest."

"So...you get to go hunting up here all the time," said Riley slowly, "and nobody can complain about all the time you're spending because it's for your book, right?"

"I guess," I responded, still unsure.

"Man!" Riley exclaimed suddenly. "I should have thought to write a book years ago! What a great scam!" The tension released as the entire crowd cracked up.

"I guess that's true," I said, finally settling into one of the mismatched wooden chairs surrounding the table. "I just happened to be the one that thought of it first."

"Well, I'm writing a book about hunting next year," Stockert announced to more laughter.

"I'll be done with hunting by then," I said. "Think anyone would want to read a book about going to Steeler games? It could be called 'A Season at Heinz Field.'"

"The hell with the Steelers," growled someone else. "I'm going to write a book about going to strip clubs. I'd just tell my wife, 'Honey, I don't want to go to the Dollhouse tonight, but I have to. You know, it's for the book.'"

And so, with the preliminaries out of the way, we launched into a late night of BS. As usual with camp conversation, it covered a variety of subjects, but most centered in some way around hunting. There was a lengthy discourse on the topic of deer population management in the Keystone State, centered mostly on the allocation of antlerless licenses (Too many? Too few?), the impact of antler restrictions (Is three points to a side too high? Too low?), and the overall whitetail herd (Too big? Too small?).

We also touched on past hunting successes and failures, the excellent play of the Steelers and their amazing rookie quarterback Ben Roethlisberger, and the history of Camp Stockert and how it came to be where it currently sits. Somewhere between extremely late at night and awfully early in the morning, we finally got around to discussing bear hunting and our plan of attack for the next day.

It first needs to be explained that black bear hunting in Pennsylvania is undertaken in a manner quite different than in other parts of North America. For starters, none of the aids available to hunters in other locales – things like bait, dogs, and spring seasons – are legal here. As a result, most hunters eschew traditional bruin strategies, such as stand hunting or spot-and-stalk, for a more straightforward approach.

According to PGC Land Management Officer George Miller, a group of guys to push through the thickest cover is one of the biggest factors in getting a bear in PA. Miller says that the most consistently successful groups have 10 to 15 hunters that "get into the woods and move bears."

Thus the classic Pennsylvania bear hunt: a half-dozen guys stationed at one end of a brush patch or rhododendron/mountain laurel thicket while another dozen storm toward them through the dense vegetation. If a bear pops out of the thicket, it's greeted by a volley from brush guns that are heavy on lead and light on subtlety: .30-.30s, .444s, and the occasional .45/70. It's unquestionably a rough shooting sport.

The reason you need an entire militia armed with guns chambered in howitzer is that "[h]unters tend to be more successful in *really* thick habitat." So says the PGC's state bear biologist, Mark Ternent. "That's where the bears are," he states flatly. "The thicker the cover, the more security they feel, especially after some hunting pressure." And in the densely regenerating clearcuts, choked out swamps, and laurel patches of the Allegheny, there is plenty of bruin security to be had.

Evidence of this is that the PGC's Miller and Wildlife Conservation Officer Mario Piccirilli had to place what amounted to a want ad for bear hunters in the agency's monthly magazine, *Pennsylvania Game News*. They are looking for more hunters in and around the Allegheny to drive down a black bear population that has led to a skyrocketing number of nuisance complaints in recent years.

Miller speculates that a number of factors have combined to increase bear numbers on the Allegheny. For one thing, there might be too much good bear habitat. "We've got a lot of bears," says Miller, "and a lot of territory to cover to find those bears. There are so many areas where bears can be, which makes it tough for hunters."

As with many game species, the single biggest factor in finding a bruin is food availability and distribution. In Miller's words, "The only thing that bear is thinking about at that time of year is food."

When the mast crop is strong, food is plentiful on the Allegheny and there is not only a decent chance of bagging a bear, but a real opportunity to nail a monster. For example, the 2001 season produced a 428-pound bruiser from Forest County and the 2002 season topped that with a 638-pound beast, also from Forest County.

I knew from my earlier forays that the Allegheny had experienced a near total failure of the hard mast crop for the second straight year. Because Novosel and Stockert had also noticed this, we rattled around a variety of strategies and potential hunt locations. In the end, with camp captain Stockert making the final call, we decided to start by pushing a maturing clearcut on the ridge behind camp, just across the South Branch of Tionesta Creek. With a workable plan finally in place, I crept up into my spot in a top bunk.

It seemed I had barely closed my eyes when I was awakened by Novosel rumbling around the kitchen, pursuing his duties as camp cook. At Camp Stockert, as Captain Ken explained to me later, "every guy has a role." Novosel pursues his with relish – not to mention maple syrup and thick slabs of real butter.

Though I had gorged myself at my premature Turkey Day meal less than 12 hours before, I couldn't resist refilling on manhole-sized pancakes and bacon strips that seemed as long and thick as my forearm. I was trying not to look too much the swine on my first day in camp, but when I saw that Novosel's griddle was outpacing us, I bore down and my fork flew.

In the end, time ran out on our pre-dawn gluttony and there was a small stack of pancakes left. I'm proud to announce, though, that the bacon supply was completely demolished.

Besides the volume and quality of the food supply, I was also surprised at the seeming lack of urgency around camp this morning. Taking their cue from the camp captain, who was still lounging on his couch-bed as the rest of us shoveled down breakfast, everyone seemed to be in slow motion, in no particular hurry to get into the woods. By the time we finalized the logistics of who would stand, who would drive, and who would ride with whom, the sun was already peeking over the ridge where we would soon be hunting.

For the first drive we posted three standers along a gas well road while the other four of us pushed the ridge toward them. I was among the drivers and we dropped down over the ridge, walking along a shallow drainage to set up the drive.

When we reached the first bench, Novosel took up his spot. Riley and I continued further down the hollow. A hundred or so yards downhill, Riley turned to me and said, "Why don't you stop here." As usual, it was an instruction, not a question.

He waved at the hillside in front of me and said, "You'll want to walk out along there. Jeff will be on that bench above you, but you probably won't be able to see him. I'll be about 100 or 150 yards below you. You'll be able to see me at first, until the ridge widens out and we get up into the clearcut – then you won't be able to see anything." I nodded.

"Just keep heading that direction," he said, sweeping his arm in front of me again. "If you get turned around, you have the radio."

The area we were driving was probably several hundred acres and over a mile long, and it was immediately clear why the PGC's Miller had suggested double the number of hunters that we had in our party. The standers – Mike and Jim Lacey and Paraska – were stretched out a couple of hundred yards apart and since they couldn't see each other there was no way they could be sure a wily bruin wouldn't sneak between them. Further, when the four drivers reached the thicker brush, the 100 or so yards between us might as well have been 100 miles. Most of the time we couldn't see or hear each other walking and, even with the handheld radios that Riley and Novosel had handed out that morning, maintaining a straight drive line was an impossibility. Despite our planning efforts and the knowledge that the camp veterans had of the terrain, the drive was uneven enough that any bear that chose to simply hunker down when we approached could have let us just waltz on by.

Still, we had to play the hand we were dealt. I stood silently, facing north and awaiting the start call on the radio. Those few minutes let me take in a small piece of the stark beauty of the skeletal forest, reduced now November's palette of browns, blacks, and a hundred hues of gray.

The dawn had come with temperatures in the low 30s, cold, but not frigid for this time of year. I was wearing my Woolrich red and black plaid wool hunting coat, purchased a dozen years ago from a widow whose departed husband, God rest his soul, had a taste for classic hunting apparel to go with his a 48-inch chest. I had also opted for my brush pants instead of the wool hunting pants I wear in colder weather. I was concerned about being overheated and about being weighed down – we were going to be doing a lot of hoofing.

I was lost in pondering the curls of my misty breath on the chill air when Stockert's voice crackled from my breast pocket. "OK, let's go," he ordered.

As Riley had forecast, the oak/cherry/maple forest was fairly open around us for the first part of the drive and I could see him most of the time. Other than a few blown over tree tops and boulder shelters, this didn't look much like black bear cover, but as the ridge widened in front of me and I climbed it sidelong, we entered a dense thicket of maple and cherry saplings. Knowing that this type of bear hunting often provides equal shooting opportunities for both standers and drivers, I unslung my .35 caliber Marlin 336 – a brush gun if there ever was one – and prepared in case a quick shot was needed.

As it turned out, no shots, quick or otherwise, were necessary. Although I came across some bear scat within the thickest part of the clearcut (though it looked to be a couple of days old, it caused me to grip the stock of the Marlin tighter), the only animals I saw were the grouse that flushed occasionally ahead of me. And the five or six other hunters that we found posted along the length of our drive.

When we finally reached the rendezvous point with our standers, Stockert griped that the unknown hunters sitting in on our drive "just posted there because they knew somebody was going to be driving that ridge." One of the many pitfalls of public land hunting in the East.

As we stood together at the end of the drive bemoaning our luck on the first drive and pondering our next move, first one then another flock of snow geese sailed high overhead, croaking out their distinctive cry. "Where are they all headed?" I wondered aloud.

"They're probably flying into the Kinzua Reservoir," Riley answered. "It's just right over there," he said, point to the north, "and it's not frozen over yet."

"Really?" I asked in surprise. "I didn't realize we were that close."

"Did you see the sign for the Red Bridge Recreation Area that we passed on the way up here this morning?" asked Stockert.

"No," I answered. "I was too busy making sure you guys didn't lose me."

Chuckling, Stockert said, "OK, then, you know where we turned onto the dirt road?" I nodded. "Well, that bridge we crossed right before that goes over Kinzua Creek. The South Branch of the Kinzua, that's the creek that runs right behind camp. Where the South Branch and the Kinzua come together, that's basically the southern limit of the reservoir. On the left side of that bridge is the Red Bridge Recreation Area."

I was fairly sure that I had heard the name Red Bridge before, but I couldn't immediately recall the significance. Later, though, I found that the spot where we stood that morning directly overlooked a nearly perfect rectangle of red pine trees, neatly laid out in rows. It was unmistakable evidence that Red Bridge had once been the site of a CCC camp, one of the most important conservation efforts ever undertaken in the US.

The Civilian Conservation Corps, one of the first of President Franklin Roosevelt's New Deal jobs programs, only lasted from 1933 to 1942. But during that relatively brief existence, this popular and widely-acclaimed program left a massive legacy across the nation by taking more than three million young men from the ranks of the jobless and planting more than three billion trees across a devastated landscape, most of those on National Forests.[28]

At the outset of his famous first Hundred Days in office, Roosevelt called an Emergency Session of Congress on March 9, 1933. He signed the bill that would create the CCC on the last day of March, and the first inductee was enrolled on April 7, just 37 days after the presidential inauguration.[29]

By September of 1935, there were half a million CCC "boys" in 2,600 camps spread to the farthest reaches of the American landscape. Over time, "Roosevelt's Tree Army," as they came to be known, had a dramatic effect upon that landscape. On eastern National Forests, the camps were plopped down among a wasteland of cut-over land, timber slashings, contaminated streams, and recurring forest fires.

But it was exactly these problems that Roosevelt envisioned his CCC forces battling. In one of his famous radio addresses to the nation, FDR directed the following statement to the boys of the CCC: "Since the Corps began some 1,150,000 of you have been graduated...Our records show that the results achieved in the protection and improvement of our timbered domain, in the arrest of soil wastage, in the development of needed recreational areas, in wildlife conservation and in flood control have been as impressive as the results achieved in the rehabilitation of youth. Through your spirit and industry it has been demonstrated that young men can be put to work in our forests, parks, and fields on projects which benefit both the nation's youth and conservation generally."[30]

Over the course of their existence, the CCCs spent more than 7 million man-days on conservation activities such as wildlife habitat protection, stream improvement, fish stocking, and the construction of small dams for public fishing and swimming.[31] In addition, the boys of the CCC planted those three billion trees to control soil erosion, a problem that was rampant during the Great Depression's Dust Bowl days.

The Red Bridge CCC camp, one of 16 on the Allegheny, was responsible for "timber surveys, forest stand improvement, establishment of forest plantations [like the one near Camp Stockert]...and seed gathering."[32] The Red Bridge boys also engaged in a war on tree-damaging porcupines and built 26 miles of trails that "parallel streams and prove a boon to sportsmen, hunters, and fisher-folk."[33] Other CCC camps left lasting marks upon the Allegheny too, such as the Ludlow camp that surveyed and constructed the dam at the Twin Lakes Recreation Area that still stands today.

According to CCC historian Mike Schultz, Fire suppression "was by far the most important contribution of the CCCs." In its nine short years of existence, the CCC built 3,470 fire towers, cut out 97,000 miles of fire roads, and spent more than 4.2 million man-days fighting fires. Among the dozens of fire-fighting and prevention projects undertaken on the Allegheny, the Red Bridge brigade rebuilt and manned the Coal Knob Lookout and boys from the Ludlow camp built a fire break around the virgin timber of the Tionesta Tract.[34]

As Schultz explains it, the area that is now the Allegheny National Forest had been in a continuous cycle of wildfires for over three decades by the time the CCC was formed. Schultz once wrote that "these fires sadly became a fixture in peoples' lives. Folks feared the coming of fire season as much as the arrival of a diphtheria, scarlet fever, or a whooping cough epidemic. Just as with these diseases, little could be done about forest fires except to hope that they would not happen to you."[35]

When I spoke to Schultz, he enlightened me a little further on the forest fire situation. "There was all this fuel built up from when they logged it down to nothing for the wood chemical industry. There was almost no green timber and piles of slashings 10 and 15 feet deep. They were just giant piles of kindling."

With this much tinder lying about the forest floor, fires started from almost any spark: lightning, logging locomotive smokestacks or brake sparks, and errant cigarettes. Or, as Shultz suggested, a more sinister source. "It was not uncommon," he said, "at a time when there were a lot of unemployed people around, for an unemployed person who was called in to fight a fire to toss a shovelful of coals 30 feet across a fire break and – Voila! – we have work for tomorrow."

In his opinion, the regular forest fire cycle might have continued indefinitely were it not for the intervention of the CCCs. "Big fires on the old timber shows [i.e., clearcuts of over 20,000 acres] were a regular occurrence before the CCCs," Schultz said. But that changed in the early 1930s. "Pinky Marker – he was the Forest Service guy that handled the CCC boys – he said to me one time that they had enough CCC boys that 'we could call them out to piss out a fire if we had to.'" From the inception of the CCCs until today, Schultz noted, the Allegheny never had a fire bigger than 500 acres.

Before that, "they were calling it the 'Allegheny Desert,'" Schultz said, "They thought it might never grow back because of the fires. I really give a lot of credit to the CCCs. By controlling forest fires they created a good economic condition [by letting forests regrow] for people from the 1980s all the way through to today."

They weren't too bad at bringing back black bear habitat either, although our first drive was hardly proof of that. The decision was finally made to cross the road and push out a small patch of thick brush that also included some crabapple trees. I delicately encouraged this option, figuring that a shortage of hard mast might make soft mast a drawing card for the bears. This theory proved to be spectacularly wrong, as most of the trees had hardly any apples on them and the ones that did had none of the clues bears usually leave behind, like claw marks and broken branches.

At the end of this drive we bumped into a PGC officer checking on bear hunters. We pressed him for some suggestions on bear hunting hotspots and he volunteered two nearby locations where he had seen bears during the fall: Swede Hill and the area at the top of Forest Road 142. Swede Hill was a couple of miles west of our current location. It was one of the spots we had discussed the night before but it had been dismissed because none of the guys in camp had hunted there before and we didn't want to waste time bumbling around looking for the right habitat. That argument held sway again this morning, so we decided to move on to Forest Road 142, which both Riley and Novosel had hunted during past deer seasons.

Although it was no more than six or eight miles distant, the drive took nearly 45 minutes. Most of that time was spent navigating the numerous ruts, curves, switchbacks, and steep grades of Forest Road 142 as we climbed to the top of the mountain.

Since it wasn't quite time for lunch yet, a few of us decided to make a quick push of a nearby hollow. The Laceys had briefly stopped off at camp, so Novosel decided to wait at the parking area for them to arrive while Stockert, Paraska, Riley, and I put on the drive. The effort was fruitless, although we once again saw bear sign along the way. When we got back to the trucks, the Laceys had arrived and Jim was helping Novosel prepare lunch.

Now, my normal idea of lunch in the woods is a bottle of Mountain Dew, sometimes supplemented by some of my personal recipe deer jerky or maybe an apple. At most, I might stash a peanut butter and jelly sandwich in my vest. But the drool-inducing aroma wafting from Novosel's portable grill on the cool midday breeze did not smell remotely like a peanut butter and jelly sandwich.

When the lid came off, the grill issued forth a succulent array of gourmet hamburgers: onion, Cajun, jalapeno, and perhaps one or two other varieties that I was too dazed to record. There were also three kinds of cheese, three different flavors of buns, and an assortment of condiments that would have made a deli manager blush. Surveying the portable banquet, I regretted that I had eaten such a big breakfast.

At the first bite of my burger, any thought that I might be too full to enjoy it immediately vanished. Chasing the main course with a selection of chips, hard pretzels, and pop that Novosel produced like a magician from the back of his truck, I was quickly ready for another. In fact, at the camp cook's urging I stuffed three (OK, four) of his gourmet burgers down my gullet. I might have had more, but I already had eaten the last one.

Fighting off the sudden urge to take a nap, I joined the rest of the crew as we walked to a timber cut about a half-mile away. The cut area was fenced to keep deer out and the growth within the fence was so dense that it was difficult to see, let alone walk, more than a few feet in any one direction. Although the length of the drive was less than a half-mile, it took the better part of an hour to complete it because of the impenetrable brush.

Worse, it was all for naught. We had nothing to show for our efforts yet again.

On the march back, the grapes of our beat-up crew were beginning to sour. "We've been pushing all damn day and haven't seen a thing," said one unhappy camper.

"We haven't even heard a shot all day," chimed in someone else.

"Yeah, that's kind of strange for up here," said Stockert in a contemplative tone. "We usually hear at least a few shots."

"Well, if we'd have gotten a bear down in that patch we just pushed," said Riley, who had taken the brunt of the abuse in driving the exclosure, "I don't even know how we would have gotten it out of there."

"We'd need an ATV," offered one of the crew.

Stockert, who feels that part of his role as camp captain is to stay current on all regulations related to hunting, said, "We wouldn't be pulling it out up here with an ATV."

"Why not?" someone asked.

"Because you're not allowed to use an ATV on the National Forest during hunting season," Stockert replied.

"Why is that? You can ride up here the rest of the year."

"That I don't really know."

I found out later from Mark Conn, the Allegheny National Forest Trails Specialist, that there is a practical reason for these closures – one that has a lot less to do with hunting than with the 25,000 to 30,000 users that the Allegheny's 110-mile trail network attracts annually.

"Sure, some hunters do like solitude and want to get away from ATVs," said Conn, who is a hunter himself, "but the main reason is that riding the trails during our wet fall season would degrade the them without the opportunity to do heavy maintenance before the winter and spring seasons. We just can't afford to do that."

Conn also told me, "I'm out there a lot talking to people and, to be honest with you, I very rarely come across a hunter that wants to have their ATV out there to hunt from. I could probably count on one hand the number of people who have asked for that ATV access during hunting season."

Count Brian Mills as one finger. Mills, president of ATV Traction Inc., a local ATV club, feels that the policy of fall trail closures is not only "severely hampering the progress of responsible ATV enthusiasts," but also disenfranchising many hunters on the Allegheny.[36]

In a lengthy essay, Mills poignantly argues that the advent of ATVs for hunting use rejuvenated older hunters in his camp: "Before their ATV, they may have been unable to get that far from camp, and could never have dragged a deer from their favorite haunt. Before their ATV their stories were mere reflections of past hunting prowess..."

"I will always remember when the same 'Old Timers' stood around the campfire after returning from a successful excursion to their favorite stand on their ATV...It was as if a proud old lion had returned to the pride saying, 'You see,

I've still got what it takes, and I can still teach you youngsters a thing or two.'"

With ATV use now restricted during hunting season Mills feels, "Something is missing around the campfire now. The 'Old Timers' are gone. They are sitting in camp letting us 'young bucks' relive our hunts without them because they are too depressed about not being able to join in." He also points out that these restrictions fly in the face of USFS and PGC policies that are attempting to increase hunter activity, especially deer harvests, saying that ATV access can increase "the number of deer taken which aids in regeneration of the forest..."

Brian Hawthorne, Public Lands Director for a national Off-Highway Vehicle (OHV) advocacy group called Blue Ribbon Coalition, has a few thoughts on the subject of National Forest hunters on ATVs as well. "We all have to realize that ATVs are popular in the hunting community now. It's here."

USFS's Conn suggested that the debate over ATV use on the Allegheny is not as heated as some of the rhetoric suggests. "We've got [ATV group] partners here that we've worked with for two and a half decades," said Conn. "The Chief of the Forest Service has said that [ATV use] is a legitimate use. They're happy that were making efforts to accommodate them. We're way ahead of the curve as far as having managed OHV use on National Forests."

The Blue Ribbon Coalition's Hawthorne warns that this type of cooperation is essential because dissention can spread within the ATV community and its individual user groups – like hunters. "Environmental groups are trying to leverage hunters [who don't ride OHVs] to prohibit vehicle use everywhere," he says This observation is backed up by the fact that the Allegheny Defense Project took time out from their anti-logging campaign to bash the Forest Service proposal for the Willow Creek ATV trails in McKean County, calling it a "wreckreation project" and howling that the "Forest Service...developed an illegally segmented recreation plan which calls for ATV as the holy grail of recreation plans."[37]

These disputes are the main reason that the Blue Ribbon Coalition is lending their support to the local OHV community on the Allegheny, particularly in the development of the new Forest Plan. Hawthorne feels their continued involvement is critical.

"The Allegheny seems to be important," he says. "As you move further east [in the US], there is less and less opportunity [for OHV users]. Private land access is reducing all the time. As a result, recreational access on the National Forest is now more important. We should be able to find a reasonable balance. At the end of the day, we've got to figure out a way to provide a primitive experience and hunters that use the vehicles need to be able to have their access as well."

As the end of our bear hunting day approached and the sun began to slant sideways through the trees atop the mountain, we figured that we had time for one more drive. The spot we selected was an aging timber cut, far less dense than the one within the deer exclosure.

I took up a position on the far right wing as we started the drive. We hadn't gone into the sapling stand very far when I flushed a grouse. Naturally, because I had the Marlin in my hands instead of a shotgun, the bird seemed to rise leisurely before clearing the treetops and sailing off at an unhurried pace on the afternoon breeze. I made a mental note that the late grouse season opened up in only three weeks.

Shortly after a second grouse flush, I noticed what appeared to be a white plastic bag lying on the forest floor about 20 yards away. Veering toward the object with the intention of shoving it in my pocket, I stopped short. The plastic bag fixed me with a stare from its round black eye.

This was no piece of trash. It was a snowshoe hare, the first one I'd ever seen.

In comparison to the cottontails that I was used to, the hare appeared to be roughly the size of a German Sheppard. This one hadn't quite completed the transition from its brown fall coat to its snowy winter one yet; he was mostly white, but I could spy some brown fur still clinging to the back of his head and around his shoulders. Comically, the hare sat stone still, convinced that I wouldn't see him even though his white coat against the gray-brown forest made him stand out like a John Deere in Times Square.

Too excited not to share this discovery, I dug out my radio and told the rest of the crew that I had found a snowshoe hare. Most of them had seen, and even hunted, snowshoes around camp before so they weren't all that impressed.

Young Mike Lacey, however, hadn't seen one before and he immediately asked me to direct him to the spot. Within five minutes, we were standing on opposite sides of the hare, admiring its striking features. Mike finally decided to approach the hare and got within about 10 yards feet before it loped off through the woods.

As we walked back to the trucks after yet another bear-free drive, Mike was still relating the details of our sighting to his dad and the rest of the group. I'm sure Jim was proud to hear his son conclude, "I don't care if we didn't see any bears today. Seeing that snowshoe made the whole trip."

By this time, the late afternoon sun had dipped behind the ridge and it was time to head back to camp. I was anxious to get on the road because I wanted to stop at the bear check station on the way home. By the time I loaded my gear in the truck, however, Novosel had another mouth-watering meal simmering in the crock pot, so I delayed my departure for a few minutes more.

By the time I reached the Marienville check station it was nearly 6 PM. On this November evening the normally quiet streets of the small town were bustling. Traffic was at a standstill, and there wasn't a parking spot within three blocks of the fire hall that houses the bear check station.

Poking my head into the check station, I was met by a heady mix of odors: the pungent smell of gore left behind by dragged bear carcasses; the musky scent of the bruins' still-fresh coats; exhaust fumes from the parade of trucks that backed in to drop off their prizes for examination; the sugary aroma of a bake sale; and the warm, fleshy odor of people crowded shoulder to shoulder to watch the action. I waved briefly to the PGC's Miller, who was running the check station then dove headlong into the scrum.

The Marienville check station is one part scientific laboratory, one part awards show, and one part street festival. As the giant overhead door opens to admit each new truck or SUV to the fire truck bay, the crowd, 200 strong, presses forward to see the trophy that will issue forth. Depending upon the size and number of bruins revealed when the tailgate drops, the display is greeted with 'Ooh's and 'Aah's, murmurs of approval, or, in the case of a particularly small bear, groans of dissatisfaction.

This public referendum is set against the backdrop of scientists from the PGC and USFS hauling the heavy carcasses onto a scale then scurrying to their notebooks as they record the age, sex, and weight of each animal. After that they hustle the successful hunter to a poster-sized map to pinpoint the location where the bear met its fate. The final reckoning on each bear is then recorded on a wall-sized tote board for the entire crowd to scrutinize as they snack on apple crisp and sip black coffee sold by the Marienville Boy Scouts. It is truly an affair to behold.

For me, the check station mood was summarized this year by three elderly men who shouldered their way through the crowd to get a closer look at each newly arrived bruin. They looked to be in their mid to late seventies and seemed, in most respects, suitably dignified for their age. Except that each one of them had perched atop his noggin a fuzzy hat shaped like the head of a bear, complete with shiny eyes, a stubby nose, and a floppy tongue hanging out of its mouth.

Unable to resist, I tapped one of them on the shoulder and asked him whether they were here just to see the bears at the check station.

"Oh, no," he replied seriously. "We're up here bear hunting today and tomorrow. We didn't see any bears today so we just decided to come over to the check station this evening and see how everyone else made out."

"I see," I said, pondering how to phrase my next question tactfully. "What's with the hats?"

"The hats?" he echoed, seemingly surprised at the inquiry. "We just thought they looked good." Then he added in a serious tone, "We didn't wear them in the woods, though."

I sought out Stockert and Riley, who had also stopped to ogle the other hunters' prizes, to say my goodbyes and share a few more sour grapes. This was our only day of bear hunting and unfortunately, in what was becoming an increasingly familiar and frustrating pattern for me, it had been an unproductive one.

With the opening day of rifle season for deer now less than a week away, it was a pattern I was hoping to shatter.

CHAPTER 9

TRADITIONS

The natural world moves in an immutable, perpetual rhythm. Seasons change; snow and rain fall; leaves bud and grow, then dry and tumble; young animals are born, mature, and then succumb, perhaps after nurturing young themselves.

Hunters have, by definition, taken on a role in the natural world – the basic and vital role of predator. As a result, we find ourselves subject to this rhythm in a way that those who choose not to hunt can never be.

Non-hunters may observe nature. They may surround themselves with nature, even immerse themselves in it, and they may take pleasure in the natural world in a very personal way. But when we choose to pursue the hunt, to literally still a beating heart, we are no longer in nature. We are *of* nature.

And yet, because we remain synchronized with the human world, we have the pleasure of knowing tradition. We have the capacity to take an object, a place, a date, and attach a significance to it that strengthens rather than diminishes with the passage of time.

The act of hunting is its own tradition, one that has been given forth to us by untold generations of our ancestors. In our ever-driven way, we have continually refined and improved the tools of the hunt, but the essence of man pursuing animal within its element remains.

Smaller and more personal traditions have also arisen around the hunt in each era of mankind. In ancient societies, a successful hunt might require a ritual offering of thanks to a god or goddess. In others, a shock of hair, or a piece of bone or horn, might be collected and worn by the hunter as a symbol of prowess. The significance of these customs may seem odd or remote to outsiders, but each repetition deepens the magnitude of their importance for those who practice them.

In Pennsylvania, most hunting traditions center on a single game species: the white-tailed deer. While this statement may hold true elsewhere as well, it resonates a bit more in a state that annually sends an orange-clad army of one million deer hunters into the woods.

One of the unyielding traditions of deer hunting in Pennsylvania is that the rifle season – usually just called "buck season" or "buck," as in, "Are you going out on the first day of buck?" – opens on the Monday after Thanksgiving. I suspect a survey would show that most of us believe this was chiseled in the fine print of Moses' tablets. As a result, schools are closed, businesses shuttered, and normally bustling streets away from the deer woods take on an eerie quiet.

The force of this tradition is such that, when the last Thanksgiving drumstick is plucked, the last pie crumb is scooped mouthward, and the last pigskin is kicked, the thoughts of a million men, women, and teens turn as one to the whitetail forests and fields. This phenomenon has been so long in place that it's hard now to know whether our expectations rise and our senses heighten because we perceive the natural world's rhythm or because our awareness of tradition compels us.

The arrival of that last weekend in November triggers its own subset of rituals. While much of the nation busies itself with mall crowds and Black Friday savings, Pennsylvania hunters prepare to become of nature once again. For tens, perhaps hundreds, of thousands of us, this means packing the guns and gear, and heading to camp. While the ritual varies from place to place and family to family, this migration from the cities and suburbs toward the remotest parts of the state often begins on the day after Thanksgiving and lasts all weekend long.

Pennsylvania hunting camps range from tarpaper-sided shacks to palatial log homes. Most of the hundreds of camps in and around the Allegheny National Forest fall somewhere in between: wooden frame or concrete block structures, usually one-story, with a low roof and a meat pole near the driveway to hang that trophy buck. Many are heated only by a fireplace or woodstove and, while most have electricity and plumbing, a surprising number still have a wooden shack out back with a half-moon on the door.

Another tradition is that hunting camp owners are obliged to give their home away from home a name, preferably one showing the personality of both the camp and its owner. Some, like my uninspired hunting mates, simply glue the word 'Camp' onto the surname of the owner, thus arriving at "Camp Stockert" or "Camp Brophy." Other camp monikers from the Allegheny, as indicated by their obligatory roadside signs, show quite a bit more imagination and humor: Pap's Place, Camp Nut-N-Fancy, The Four Aces, Flatlanders Camp, Buck Snort Lodge, Rough Cut Lodge, Camp 4 Point, Lady Luck Lodge, Old Stag Camp, Rob-In Lodge, Kinzua Castle, and Tippin Inn.

My personal favorite is a camp that we discovered on a family trip to the Allegheny when I was a kid. Made of a giant piece of corrugated metal drainpipe with pieces of plywood fastened to each end, it was called Hobo Heaven. Much to my surprise, I rediscovered Hobo Heaven during one of my recent trips to the Allegheny, but disappointingly the old drainpipe had been replaced by a mobile home.

In addition to a name tag, each camp also has a history attached to it. For example, I was surprised to hear from Ken Stockert that his two-bunkroom, one-bath (*sans* running water) structure in Bliss Hill, McKean County, is now several miles from its original location.

"The camp was first built by my grandfather," Ken began proudly, as we sat with our elbows propped on the red-and-white checked tablecloth of its kitchen table. Then he stopped abruptly and corrected himself. "Well, my grandfather and one of his friends put up the money to buy the property and construct the camp. My dad and some of his friends actually built it," he said with his habitual chuckle. "That was in the mid '50s."

"It originally sat in the town of Kinzua," Ken continued, "which was just a typical northern Pennsylvania logging town. Then, when the Kinzua Dam was built in the '60s, that property, the whole town actually, was acquired by the [US Army] Corps [of Engineers]. Dad already owned the property here, so he took the money to move the structure to this location. Dad had to load the camp up on a flatbed truck and they hauled it up here." When his father passed away in 1987, Ken's mom transferred ownership to her only son.

The Camp Stockert rituals for the weekend before buck season mimic those of most other camps around the National Forest. Once everyone reaches camp, Saturday morning is traditionally given over to small game hunting. During this period, people who might not spend another minute of the year in pursuit of small game use squirrel and grouse hunting as an excuse to squeeze in just a few hours more scouting for deer.

Saturday afternoon is frequently dedicated to sighting in the deer rifle. More correctly, given that most hunters fuss over their rifles like a mother over a newborn and therefore don't need any more adjustment, the time is spent firing round after round to burn off some of the excess energy that comes from knowing that the biggest day of the year is less than 36 hours away.

Saturday evening is often the height of the social calendar. At some camps, like Camp Brophy, the evening is spent eating a huge meal cooked on the camp stove. For others, Saturday evening is a night out. The Camp Stockert crew, for example, spends the evening gnawing fat, juicy steaks at the nearby Westline Inn. Whatever the diversion, with no early wake-up required, Saturday night often stretches well into Sunday morning as hunters cluster around the table exchanging stories, drinks, and poker chips.

This ritual has given rise to a pet theory of mine: that the single most valuable and useful piece of furniture at any hunting camp is the kitchen table. I stumbled onto this notion when Dan Brophy was describing the recent renovation of a neighboring camp. Rather than focusing on the gorgeous wooden exterior of the camp or the interior décor, he said, "It's great – they have this huge kitchen table! I bet you could get about a dozen people around it!" Indeed, when it comes to camp tables, size does matter.

Perhaps the camp table is yet another tradition, one handed down to us by our medieval ancestors and the Great Halls of their castles. Or perhaps it's just a gathering place of convenience, close to the food, drinks, and, most importantly, fellow members of camp. Whatever the reason, practicality or tradition, when Sunday's breakfast lands on the table, the countdown to Opening Day begins in earnest. As Jeff Novosel says, "Everyone starts putting their game face on."

With no Sunday hunting in Pennsylvania, Sundays are often spent puttering around camp making the small fixes and cleanups that have somehow been avoided since last year. For the late arrivals or those that simply can't resist, there's an optional second round of target shooting. By Sunday evening, most of the last stragglers have made it into camp, unless, like me, they have Steeler-Redskin tickets and arrive after the rest of their campmates are in bed.

Unlike in bear season, there was no late night fat-chewing or last minute strategizing at Camp Stockert. It was deer season now and that meant serious business and an early bedtime. I slipped into my assigned bunk as quietly as possible and was almost immediately snoring like a chainsaw.

In the morning, I learned two things about Opening Day at Camp Stockert. First, the wake-up call was much earlier than it had been for bear season. It was about 4:30 AM when I first heard Novosel bouncing around the kitchen working on the morning meal. The immortal words of assistant groundskeeper Carl Spackler from *Caddyshack* ran through my mind: "I guess we're playing for keeps now. I guess the kidding around is pretty much over, huh?"

The second thing I discovered early that morning was that the cast of characters had changed from a week ago. Gone were Paraska and the Laceys, *pere et fils*. In their places were Riley's father, Bruce, a camp newcomer with the face of an Irish cherub and the same deadpan sense of humor as his son; Novosel's son, Mike, a lifetime veteran of the camp; Mike's Penn State classmate, Andy Linder, who was on his first hunting trip of any kind; Phil Bartell, another from

Ken's stockpile of brothers-in-law; and camp regular Sam Jones.

Ken had prepped me the previous week for meeting Jones. "Wait till you meet Sam," he told me, laughing a little harder than usual as he looked at Novosel and me across the rim of his Jim Beam and Coke. "He's a piece of work." Another chuckle.

"He always gets a deer, though," observed Novosel.

"Yes, he does," agreed Ken emphatically. "He gets a deer almost every year, even back when it was bucks only." Then he said seriously, "Everyone in camp has a role and Sam's job is to put meat on the pole and make sure Camp Stockert doesn't get shut out. That's his job and he's good at it."

"*Very* good at it," Novosel added.

"Yep," said Ken, punctuating the assessment with another sip of his drink. He swallowed then added, "He's still a piece of work, though."

On Opening Day, Jones rumbled out of the back bunkroom after the rest of us had taken our seats at the breakfast table. He had the disheveled and grumpy appearance of a bear awakened from its hibernation on an especially cold winter morning. He was muttering unintelligibly under his breath, when someone pointed out that I was sitting across the table from him. He brightened momentarily. "You're Rob?" he asked.

"That's me," I said as cheerfully as I could muster at that hour.

"You're the one writing the book, right?" he asked. Then without waiting for an answer, he added, "That's cool." That was followed immediately by, "Ah, man, I feel terrible. I need to get in the bathroom."

The last comment produced a round of laughter from the table as he retired to the john. The rest of us wrapped up the loose ends on where everyone would be on stand that morning. Since virtually everyone else had hunted the area for years or was teamed with someone who had, this was mostly just an effort to acquaint me with everyone's whereabouts and determine where I was going to go.

Once I knew where everyone else would be stationed, it was my turn to pick that magical spot that might bring me a wallhanger buck or a fat doe to fill my freezer. Given my limited knowledge of the area my choices were slim; they were further narrowed when I found that some of the other guys had already picked spots I was considering. I finally selected what I thought would be one of the harder areas to access by foot, the point of a ridge that jutted out of the mountainside just behind camp. I reasoned that its distance from the road would minimize the number of other hunters in the immediate vicinity, and its proximity to a brushy clearcut might make it an attractive spot for spooked deer seeking cover. As it turned out, I was exactly right on the latter point, but couldn't have been more wrong on the former.

The first hunters left at 5:40 AM; I was out the door at 5:55. I happened to follow the Rileys out and I made a point to tell Bruce, who was clad from his neck to his ankles in red and black plaid Woolrich wool coat and pants, that I liked his outfit. I pointed to my own identical coat.

"You've got the pants, too, though," I noted, and before I could say the words, he announced with a grin, "A Pennsylvania Tuxedo." The term references the hordes of Pennsylvania hunters who clothed themselves in Woolrich's familiar black-on-deep-cherry-red plaid so frequently that the full coat and pants ensemble became known as the Pennsylvania Tuxedo. Yet another Pennsylvania deer hunting tradition carried forward.

I eased the F-150 up the winding Forest Road in the dark and glided to a stop as quietly as possible. After a walk of about a mile I reached the end of the ridge, and selected a spot near the top of the nose. From here I could look back into a regenerating timber cut and also down on a bench that was covered with goldenrod. What I couldn't see from here was anything further down the mountainside than the bench.

Still, I liked the spot. Any deer that bolted for the cover of the thicket above me would have to come past me, deer driven up out of the bottom by hunters near camp would likely climb onto the shelf in front of me, and anything that tried to slip out along the edge of the ridge would walk almost directly below me. On top of that, it was a crisp 28-degree morning with no snow at all. If deer were moving I would hear them on the crunchy leaves long before they got to me.

I settled into my spot about 30 minutes before sunrise. As the woods turned from black-and-white to Technicolor on the beams of the rising sun, I could fairly smell the anticipation on the chilly air. I had a regular hunting license tag, which entitled me to take a buck with at least three points on one side, plus two antlerless tags. With high deer numbers and lots of hunters in the woods to move them, the odds were good.

I didn't have to wait long for the action to start nearby. The first shots, a three-round volley, were fired across the valley at 6:55 AM. There was sporadic shooting further away for nearly an hour before things got hot right in our neighborhood.

At 7:45 someone cut loose with several rounds off to my left, in an area the Camp Stockert guys call Big Valley. This area, Ken had advised me might be manned by hunters from what he calls "Camp Yellow Boots." He said this group – whose name was derived from the yellow rubber boots some of the camp members wear to forge the South Branch of Kinzua Creek – might have as many as a dozen hunters along the ridge.

Apparently the folks from Camp Yellow Boots were in an awful hurry to empty their guns. The first few shots on my left were followed by a series of shots coming progressively closer. The deer were running, and they were coming my way.

I pulled the Marlin .35 off my shoulder and made sure the scope was dialed down to 3x. If a deer squirted up over the ridge after running through that gauntlet of fire, it was going to be in a big hurry and I wanted as wide a field of view as possible.

I turned to get a better view of the bench on my left and waited to hear the crunch of dry leaves under hooves. Instead, I heard another two shots fired further back the ridge above me.

Either there was a new whitetail in play or the running deer had changed directions and gone up the ridge at a different spot. As I pondered this new information, I heard another shot from directly down over the front of the ridge, but several hundred yards away. That was followed by another series of volleys on my right, which told me that the shot down below had started deer running in that direction. The shooting on that side of the ridge tapered away from me so I figured those deer had circled along the ridge below my bench.

Sporadic shooting continued around me for the next hour or so, but I neither saw nor heard a single deer. At about 9 AM, I decided slip further down the ridge to a spot where I could see more of the South Branch valley below me. As it turned out, I could see quite a bit more; when I peeked out over the rim of the bench to the ridge below, I was surprised to see three hunters, perched 50 yards apart.

Revising my plan, I moved to the right side of the point, only to find two more hunters seated there, gazing down into the valley below. I was gaining a clearer picture of why I hadn't seen any deer this morning.

Looking to find someplace a little further from the crowd, but unwilling to travel too much because it was still prime shooting time, I decided to head up the point of the ridge instead of down. From here my view would be less, but at least I could hunt the thick escape cover of the timber cut.

I picked a spot that was slightly more open and sat down on an old stump. Under the circumstances I was pretty happy with the stand, which was near the intersection of a couple of well-worn deer trails. While deer may not be able to get through all the hunters coming up the slope, I reasoned, they might sneak down here from above.

Within five minutes I heard the crunch of leaves along the ridge behind me. I slowly swiveled my head in that direction to pick up movement.

It didn't take long to spot the source of the noise, especially since it was wearing safety orange. Two hunters walked up to a point about 60 yards away from me and stopped.

They were pointing and gesturing back out over the left side of the ridge, in the direction that I had heard shooting earlier. After a couple of minutes, one of the hunters turned and walked away while the remaining one took off his hunting coat.

Well, I thought in disgust, either he's getting ready to go to the bathroom or he's getting ready to gut a deer. The answer came quickly as I saw him reach down and roll a dead deer onto its back. At that moment, I would have almost rather seen him drop his pants.

The mid-morning radio check came just then and the news I heard made my blood pressure rise even higher. Everyone else from camp had at least seen a deer; three hunters – Ken, Bartell, and, of course, Jones – already had deer down. Then it was my turn to report.

"I haven't seen a damn thing," I griped, making no attempt to conceal my aggravation. "Unless you count other hunters. Christ, there's more people up here than at the mall!"

I could hear the laughter in Ken's voice as he said, "Why don't you come on down here then?"

"Here" was a spot that Ken refers to as 'The Zoo,' a triangular patch of brush and grass that sits south of the confluence of the South Branch and Kinzua Creek. "I shot a doe down here and I need to drag her out, but there were 5 or 6 other deer with her. Jeff's pretty close to me, and so are Mike and Andy, so if you come down we can all get together and drive this out. We'll see if we can find those other deer."

I quickly agreed and set out over the steep edge of the mountain. Novosel directed me over the radio to drop down until I found an abandoned logging railroad grade – a common remnant of the historic logging industry found nearly everywhere on the Allegheny – where I would turn left, parallel to the main stem of Kinzua Creek.

As I walked away from my spot, I realized that I had been sitting in the center of a ring of at least ten hunters. Later I found that the shooting I heard on my left was directed at three deer that had run through the Camp Yellow Boots skirmish line. One, a buck, had been dropped immediately. The other two, both does, had run up onto the ridge behind me. There one of them – the one that I saw being gutted – expired and the other turned 180 degrees and went back down the ridge. This turned out to be a poor choice as it was killed about 150 yards away.

The shots that I had heard in front of me, near the bottom of the ridge, were from Jones. Still not feeling well, he had been late getting into the woods. Following his usual pattern, he used waders to cross the South Branch then walked a short distance up the base of the ridge. Climbing into his treestand well after shooting light, he was still getting settled in his seat when he heard deer approaching.

"It was an easy shot," he told me later. "I just looked to see if he had enough points, then put the crosshairs on him and pulled the trigger. He fell right there."

The buck was a 6-point with a 12 ½" spread, a fairly nice rack for a deer on the Allegheny. Ken and Novosel were right – Jones is one of those guys who just always seem to get a deer.

After his shot, the two does that were with Jones' buck had cut from left to right below my first location. This accounted for the shooting that I heard on my right, although I never found out whether they had been hit.

Around the same time that Ken shot his doe in The Zoo, Bartell was moving down opposite side of the South Branch.

"I was just walking down toward the creek looking for a spot," he said afterward, "and these two bucks came walking right toward me." The bucks both sported legal antlers and they never saw Bartell as they crossed in front of him.

"I had the gun up," he said, "but I had to wait until I could get a clear shot at one of them. I couldn't see their antlers very well because they were kind of together in the scope. I just waited until one came clear and shot him." He clearly made the right choice: his buck was a heavy beamed 8-point with a 15 ½" spread, probably the largest rack ever taken out of Camp Stockert.

By 10 AM, we had a doe and two brag-worthy bucks. We knew of at least two more does and another buck killed in the immediate vicinity, and there was a good chance that one or both of the does running with Jones' buck had also been dropped. It was quite a bit of action, and when I related the details to Dave deCallesta the next day, he smiled behind his thick glasses.

"That's what we like to hear," he said warmly. "More does being killed and bigger bucks on the National Forest. That's what we're looking for."

deCallesta, a retired USFS biologist, is now working as a private consultant for the Sand County Foundation, a Wisconsin-based conservation group. The "we" that he referenced is a complex network of public and private landowners who have come together in the northeastern corner of the Allegheny National Forest to make a difference in deer populations and forest habitat. The name of the project is the Kinzua Quality Deer Cooperative, and, to the best of anyone's knowledge, it is the only one of its kind.

According to Kevin McAleese, Program Director for the KQDC, this project has roots that go back to the father of modern wildlife management, Aldo Leopold. SCF was founded by Leopold's godson, Reed Coleman. Coleman's father, Tom, was one of Leopold's closest friends and hunting partners. The area around Leopold's now famous Wisconsin "Shack," where he lived when he wrote the conservation classic *A Sand County Almanac*, was one of the areas that the pals frequented on their hunts.

Beginning in 1987, SCF's president Brent Hoaglund initiated a variety of long-term ecological research projects at the Leopold Memorial Reserve, the 1,500-acre property around the Shack property. One of the most important of those was on the impacts of browsing from an overpopulated deer herd. Based upon the results of that research, Hoaglund proposed what became known as the "Earn a Buck" program.

"Brent Hoaglund said, 'If you, the hunter, commit to killing antlerless deer at a two-to-one ratio we will protect your opening day hunting rights [on the Reserve] in perpetuity,'" explains McAleese. "The hunters in that area agreed to do it and SCF has data showing that the quality of the bucks has continued to go up. They're finding older deer, the deer are heavier, and they have bigger antlers."

Because of the success of the program, SCF started a three-year seminar series in 1996 with the intention of sharing their experiences at the Reserve. Shortly after that, Dr. Susan Stout contact SCF to begin similar work on the Allegheny.

The documented damage from browsing on the Tionesta Tract, as well as the continuing need to fence regenerating timber cuts to protect them from deer is strong evidence of the need for better whitetail management on the Allegheny. What most people fail to realize, though, is that this is hardly news. Biologists and land managers have been complaining about habitat damage from deer overabundance since at least 1931, when the PGC, over the objections of many hunters, instituted a special combined antlered and antlerless season on the Allegheny.[38]

A 1940 report on deer hunting and populations on the National Forest states, "The size of the deer herd...must be kept in balance with the amount of food available to support it."[39] A 1958 report says that "Since deer are dependent upon forests for survival, it behooves us to manage deer numbers so that the forests' production of deer food can be maintained along with a reasonable deer herd."[40] And again, in 1960: "Some hunters would like to believe that there is no limit to the number of deer which can be supported. Deer must eat, and the herd must be held within the bounds of its natural food supply...[I]t would be foolhardy to allow overutilization, which would result in...fewer and poorer quality deer in the future."

The dire tone of these warnings, and the need to repeat them every decade, hints at yet another tradition of Pennsylvania deer hunting – mistrust between hunters and the scientific community that attempts to regulate the harvest. That battle rages on today, as indicated by a July 2005 column in *Field and Stream*, entitled "The Deer Wars."[41] In it, recently retired PGC deer program director Dr. Gary Alt says, "The areas where [deer numbers exploded] in the 1930s – the north-central counties – now have the lowest deer densities. There is no understory there."

Countering Alt's position in the article is Greg Levengood, chairman of a group called Unified Sportsmen of Pennsylvania. Levengood says that the recent changes in deer management – primarily antler restrictions and increased antlerless license allocations – are "guaranteed to kill hunting." He contends that the poor habitat conditions and lack of forest understory are due to acid rain, not an overpopulation of deer. "We have the highest acid rain deposition in the country, and a forest canopy in places where sunlight can't hit the ground. Under those conditions it looks like deer overbrowsed," says Levengood.

This theory, of course, fails to explain why young forest stands inside deer exclosures – such as the one we encountered during bear season – grow back so thick and dense that an ant would have to turn sideways to squeeze through, while areas outside the fence have little vegetation except ferns, one of a whitetail's least favorite foods. Perhaps the fences somehow keep out the acid rain.

Given the festering unrest over deer management in Pennsylvania, SCF's McAleese realized quickly that they would need a team of strong partners if they were to institute a program on the heavily hunted Allegheny. What resulted was nearly 75,000 acres of mostly forested property, some federal land (about 48,000 acres on the Allegheny), some owned by local government (about 12,000 acres), and some held by private timber companies (about 13,000 acres). It's that size and mix of landownership that makes the KQDC unique.

Tim Lilley, of the Georgia-based Quality Deer Management Association, explained to me that there are numerous Quality Deer Management programs larger than the KQDC across the US. But, said Lilley, "The KQDC is undoubtedly the most unique Quality Deer Management cooperative in terms of land ownership makeup."

QDMA Executive Director Brian Murphy takes Lilley's comments a step further. "To the best of my knowledge," says Murphy, "the KQDC is the *only* Quality Deer Management project involving National Forest property."

As USFS wildlife biologist Scott Reitz explains in a research paper published last summer, the true goal of the KQDC is to "change forest regeneration and renewal at the landscape level."[42] Beyond that, he told me when we spoke, "We're trying to reduce the deer herd, but improve the quality of deer *hunting* on the KQDC area."

Although some hunters gripe about the regulation changes and additional license allocations, somebody is buying all those tags: Wildlife Management Unit 2F (which includes the Allegheny) took barely a week to become the first WMU in the state to sell out and the 5,000 additional tags made available for the KQDC were gone by August 15. I managed to get one of the regular antlerless tags for WMU 2F, but got shut out of the KQDC tags.

The KQDC partners have worked hard to create perks for participating hunters. They staff the voluntary deer check stations, where successful hunters can learn the age and weight of their deer and compare them to others taken in the vicinity. In keeping with SCF's 2-for-1 theme, successful KQDC hunters get two raffle tickets for each doe they check and one for each buck. These tickets are redeemable for door prizes at the annual KQDC banquet in February, which this year attracted 169 hunters, despite being held during a driving snowstorm.

This "grand experiment," as McAleese calls the KQDC, started with the 2001 hunting season and is slated to last for at least ten years. Nearing the halfway point, some progress is evident. For example, spring pellet counts have shown that deer densities within the KQDC have gone down the past two years.

Another measure of the program's success – and an early indicator that the forest habitat is rebounding – is the weight of the deer recorded at the check stations. When I spoke to deCallesta at the Westline Inn check station on the second day of rifle season, one of the first things he said to me was, "They're definitely bigger this year." To back that up he shared the following data: Adult male deer weights have gone from a 115-pound average (field dressed) in 2001 to 122 pounds in 2003 to 126 pounds for the ones he had checked at that point of the 2004 season. The trend for adult does followed their male counterparts closely, going from a 100-pound average in 2001 to 107 pounds in 2004. "The trend is very encouraging," said deCallesta.

McAleese put it another way: "Our vision is to make hunters on these public areas forest stewards and part of the forest restoration effort. It's a way to engage people who have traditionally only been resource users in the management process. I'm not aware of another effort like it." Then, he added, "This is groundbreaking. We're quite proud to be involved in it."

Back on the mountain, as I slipped and skidded my way down the face of the ridge toward The Zoo, I wasn't thinking about banquets or raffles, although questions about deer populations were definitely on my mind. Specifically, I was wondering, Where in the hell are they? And why is everyone else seeing them except me?

Within minutes I got a partial answer to the first question when two does bounded up out of the ferns about 60 yards below me. I snapped the Marlin to my shoulder but by the time I got my footing and found them in the scope, they were nothing more than a pair of bouncing tails far in the distance.

About 15 minutes later I met up with the two Novosels and Linder. We quickly recounted the deer we had seen that morning and lamented the fact that none of us had been able to get a shot off. Then we moved off toward The Zoo, where we ran into Ken dragging out his doe. He quickly gave us the details of his successful morning then returned to the task of getting the deer to the meat pole.

With Linder and me standing, Jeff and Mike drove out The Zoo, but there were no deer to be seen. From here, we doubled back to the south and Jeff and I drove out the old

CCC pine plantation for Mike and Linder. Again, we came up empty.

The next move for the four of us was to hunt our way out the tram road to Jeff's vehicle because mine was still parked on the ridge above us. We started out on the abandoned railroad grade, but it was so narrow that we had to proceed two-by-two behind each other. This formation seemed somewhat impractical, especially when Mike mentioned that deer often bolt across the old grade. If that happened, at least two of us would have no safe opportunity to shoot.

After a few minutes of marching in formation and eyeballing the steep ridge on my right, I finally announced that I was going to climb back up the hillside to my truck. This drew some odd looks and disapproving comments from the other three (I think "You're nuts" was one of them), but my mind was made up. I slung the Marlin over my shoulder and started the ascent.

Walking down the hill an hour earlier had been difficult due to the many downed branches, wobbly rocks, and crumbling soil loosened by the weeks of recent rain. Hauling my sweating carcass up the face of it now – naturally, I had picked an even steeper section to climb than the one I came down – became a near heart attack-inducing test of will. I hadn't gone 20 yards up hill when I had to slide my rifle sling completely over my neck and shoulders. Then at least I was able to proceed by crawling on my hands and knees and grasping each tiny sapling, jutting rock, or downed log to pull myself to the next foothold. With the damp soil giving way every few seconds, it was like climbing up an amusement park waterslide wearing felt pack boots and carrying 20 pounds of clothing and gear.

By this time, the outside temperature had risen to a rather pleasant 35 degrees. Pleasant, that is, if you weren't scaling a cliff. I tore open the buttons on my heavy Woolrich coat and on the wool shirt that I wore beneath, but that barely began to vent the heat that my furnace was generating. Taking the coat and heavy shirt off wasn't an option either because I had no way to carry them; I needed both hands free to drag myself uphill.

At last, with my body temperature approaching molten lava level, I reached a flat spot where I could stop to determine whether my lungs and heart were still inside my chest. As I wheezed like a four-pack a day smoker in a marathon, I glanced up to see Bruce – we had taken to jokingly calling him "Father Riley" – grinning down at me from near the top of the hill, still 100 yards away. I mustered a half-wave then threw my head back to suck some more sweet, cool air into my burning torso. When I felt that the severe aneurysm danger had finally passed, I lumbered the rest of the way up to where Bruce stood.

"That's a tough walk," he said unnecessarily.

"Please shoot me," I panted back.

Apparently mistaking my request for a joke, Bruce laughed quietly and then recounted his morning events for me. From what I could hear over the hammering of my heart, it sounded like he had seen just one deer, early in the morning, but couldn't get a shot.

I told him that we were getting together to put on some drives and invited him along, but he declined, saying simply, "No, thanks. I like to stand."

Telling Father Riley that I'd check back with him later, I headed to the truck and drove down the mountain. The location for our next drive was a hardwood swamp along the north bank of Kinzua Creek that the Camp Stockert gang calls the Okefenokee Swamp. Perhaps because I still looked like a potential candidate for arterial thrombosis, I was elected to be one of the standers on this drive so I took up the post nearest the creek.

The drive took about 45 minutes and didn't produce a deer. Mike Novosel was the driver that came out closest to me and we gabbed briefly as we walked back toward the road and the rest of the group. As he strolled a few steps ahead of me, my attention was drawn to a small patch of beech saplings at the edge of the swamp. I had barely altered my course to move toward the saplings when a doe burst volcanically from the copse and rocketed back toward the swamp. The Marlin was quick to my shoulder, but not quick enough – two jumps into the thick undergrowth and she was invisible again.

We once again debated our next move. The sun was already moving low along the tree line above us, so decisions were becoming more critical. As the camp veterans debated the merits of places I had never heard of, my eyes wandered to a patch of land on the opposite side of a logging road from the Okefenokee. The area held a mix of overgrown crabapple trees, alder thicket, and goldenrod on the higher hummocks. It looked pretty deer-y to me.

"What do you guys think about driving that out?" I asked. There was muted mumbling, as though I had suggested tapping a keg during Sunday church service.

"We don't usually drive that piece," said Novosel slowly.

"I don't think we've ever driven it," Ken tacked on. "You think we should try it?"

"Well, you guys know the area a hell of a lot better than I do," I said, "But that looks like pretty good deer habitat."

The mumbling had turned to thoughtful silence. "Plus," I added, sensing the momentum swinging my way, "if you guys don't drive it, that probably means everybody else leaves it alone too."

That sealed the deal. "Let's give it a shot," announced Ken with his usual enthusiasm. "If it doesn't work, we'll have Rob to blame for wasting the afternoon."

After some quick planning, we started the drive. I was on the far left wing, following the north bank of the Kinzua. On my right was Bartell, who still had an antlerless tag to fill and was attempting to do so with a flintlock muzzleloader, which he was trying out for the first time.

When we passed the stand of crabapples, we came into a series of dry or mostly dry channels that had been cut by the creek over the years. Each channel was about eight or ten feet deep, maybe 15 or 20 feet wide, with banks choked in thick alders. As I crested the bank of the second channel, I saw ear tips disappear around a bend about 50 yards ahead of me.

"Phil," I hissed, "There're deer up there. Right in front of us."

"What do you want to do?" he asked after a moment.

"Let's just keep moving ahead," I replied. "Hopefully they'll go right to Mike and Andy. Be ready though. In this thick stuff we could come right up on them."

We walked the next 75 yards as stealthily as possible. The rushing stream covered our sound, but the wind was swirling here in the bottom of the valley.

I crested another channel bank and saw the tail of a deer bounding off to my right, heading toward the rest of our drivers. Deciding the time for stealth had passed, I shouted, "There's one running – coming up the hill!"

A few seconds later, a shot thundered from Jeff Novosel's inline muzzleloader, but the only thing he hit was a three-inch sapling. I could hear deer scrambling in all directions through the alders ahead of me and excited shouting from the other hunters.

It abruptly dawned on me that the deer were either going to be hemmed in by our drive or they were going to bolt from the trap by the only escape route we had left them – crossing Kinzua Creek. Trying to keep them bottled up, I swung out to my left and into the stream.

This section of Kinzua Creek is actually a series of gravelly channels separated by tiny islands and sand bars. Some of the channels run with four or five inches of water, others have no flow at all. Since I was still wearing only my 10-inch felt pack boots, I tried to stick to the shallower draws.

I crept slowly through the ankle-deep water, trying to use the brush on the little islands and bars as cover. As I rounded the tip of one brushy spit, I looked downstream and saw something move around the end of the next island. I strained my eyes to get a better look. A waving branch? No, wait, a twitching ear!

The doe's head seemed to materialize in a split second. In another split second, I had the crosshairs of the Bushnell scope on her.

I couldn't see anything beyond the doe's head. I decided to wait for her to step out into the channel where I would have a clear sight line and could line up a shoulder shot.

The doe turned to look back over her shoulder. I used that instant to move two steps to my left so that I could see around a single branch that jutted between us. It was a crucial mistake.

As I swung the scope back up to my eye, she was already bolting across the main channel, splashing through the haunch-deep water at full speed. Jolted, I cracked off a terrible shot that I knew instantly was a miss.

Steadying myself, I swung the rifle back to the right hoping to find another deer following her. And I did.

One galloping deer after another sailed through my scope in a series of brown blurs. I had no choice but to keep panning to the right until I found one that I could get my sights on.

Finally the scope settled onto a doe that had just splashed down off of the bank. She was moving quickly, but I locked the crosshairs onto her shoulder and swung the rifle to the left as she ran. Just as she reached a midstream gravel bar I took the shot.

It was a running shot from 80 yards away...while standing in rushing water. Though the doe disappeared, I thought there was a decent chance I had hit her, and told Ken and Bartell so when they rushed over to meet me.

Now, though, we faced a dilemma. The deer, with one possibly wounded, were on one side of Kinzua Creek and we were on the other. We had less than an hour of daylight left and only Ken was wearing waders.

After kicking around our options, it was agreed that Bartell would join the rest of the crew, who were still following up on Novosel's shot. From there they would head back to camp.

Ken would wade to the south side of the stream and look for signs of a hit on the gravel bar and opposite bank. I, meanwhile, would stand on the north bank and look on in frustration.

I adhered to the terms of that arrangement until Ken held something aloft and shouted, "I found some hair!"

"Really?!" I yelled back.

"Yep, a tuft of white hair right here on the gravel bar," he said, pointing to a spot at his feet.

"That's where she was when I shot," I replied, my excitement rising. "She jumped out of the stream right there."

"Well, it looks like you hit her," he said. Looking in a circle, he added, "But I don't know where she went from here."

It was more than I could take. "The hell with this," I said. "I'm coming over there. It's only a little water and it's not that goddam cold out here." Ken fairly bawled with laughter as I slogged across the knee-deep creek. The insulation in my boots was instantly so drenched that I felt like I was wearing cement blocks on my feet.

"It could be worse," Ken said, launching into a story about how he and Sean Riley had crossed the Kinzua in sub-zero temperatures one year. Truthfully, I wasn't listening. I was thinking only of finding my deer.

Like seemingly everything else that had happened while hunting this fall, the search ended badly for me. We scoured the banks of the stream and eventually found the place where the herd of deer had climbed out, but we never found so much as a drop of blood. Nothing except that single clump of hair.

Apparently my shot had just creased the running doe, either skimming her stomach or, more likely, nipping her chest because I swung the rifle a bit too quickly. Either way, hunting on the Allegheny was turning into a season of frustration for me.

As anyone who knows me can attest, I am, by any standard, a poor loser. And now, with the weight of one unsuccessful trip to the Allegheny after another piling upon my back, I had missed a somewhat difficult but still achievable shot on a National Forest prize.

I was both aggravated and discouraged when we got back to camp. Even another of Novosel's fantastic meals wasn't enough to raise me out of my sullen mood.

In actuality, it had been a fairly successful day for the camp: we had bagged three deer, including Phil's impressive buck, and every one of us either had a shot or had a deer in his sights. We were all staying over to hunt the morning too. But in my current mood, the prospects did not seem promising.

The next morning brought a change in strategy from the first. We started with a couple of small drives around the confluence of the South Branch and Kinzua Creek, near where I had missed the previous evening. These turned up nothing, so we decided to take another crack at driving the Okefenokee.

We dropped off three standers at the downstream end of the swamp then moved to the head of it. We were about to begin when we encountered another group of hunters putting on their own drive through the swamp.

With the rest of our troop already at their posts, we were reluctant to give up. Instead we decided to wait a bit to let the other party clear out of the swamp; then we would proceed with our drive as intended. As we swung our legs from the truck tailgates, someone suggested killing a few minutes by driving out the small piece of swamp upstream of where we sat.

Ken took Mike Novosel and Linder to the upstream end of the marshy patch while Jeff and I covered the lower end. As I looked for a spot to stand, I knew my location would be a headache because the vegetation around me was chest-high. Any deer moving in here was going to be nearly impossible to see, let alone shoot.

I looked for a higher vantage point on the hillside, but overhanging hemlock branches made the sightlines even worse from there. Finally, with the now all-too-familiar feeling of frustration beginning to creep in, I picked a spot on a slight rise and hoped for the best.

Naturally, the best did not happen. Not long after the drive started, I heard movement in the grass out in front of me. As the sound approached, I followed it until I finally spotted the source – two does loping through the tall grass. I had no chance at a shot because I could only see the tops of their heads as they crested each leap, so they rocketed within 20 yards of me unmolested.

I followed their noisy escape until I caught a brief glimpse of them behind me. Between the overhanging hemlock branches I could see that they were climbing the bank that led to the road – if they reached it, they would be gone for good.

I jumped up and hustled off to my right about 20 yards. When I stopped to scope the pair, there was no clear shot to be had. My view through the scope was a jumble of legs, shoulders, and hemlock needles. Desperate, I dialed the scope up to 7x magnification.

That only helped a little. At least now I could tell what was deer and what was tree, but I was still having trouble picking out a vital spot.

To make matters worse, I was aiming up at the does, who were about 60 yards away and about 25 feet above me. Another tough shot.

I took it. At the crack of the rifle, both deer launched themselves over the crest of the bank and out of my sight. When neither of them fell, an unwanted feeling crept into the bottom of my gut.

I climbed quickly up the hill and ran into Mark Heider, a sometime Camp Stockert occupant, who had just arrived for the day's hunt with his young son, Matt. Before he introduced himself, Heider asked, "Was that you that shot?" When I said that it was, he replied, "Well, you hit one of those deer."

"Are you sure?" I inquired quickly.

"Yeah," he said with certainty. "It was dragging a leg when it crossed the road."

This was hardly the best news I could have gotten, but it was far from the worst. As Heider and I scoured the road surface for blood, Ken and the rest of the crew arrived.

I gave a hurried explanation of what happened. When I finished, Ken snickered as he said, "So you missed again?" I resisted the urge to shoot him where he stood.

"Maybe," I replied noncommittally, "although Mark says he thinks I hit it."

"Did you find any blood?" asked Ken.

"Um...well..." I stammered.

Ken laughed again. "OK," he said, ever the camp captain. "They went into the swamp, right?" That we could agree on. "Then let's go ahead and drive it out like we were going to do anyway."

And so, on his command, we spread out across the swamp and moved in. I was assigned to follow the trail of the two deer through the muddy leaves.

Although there were occasional scuffs in the leaf litter that might have come from a wounded deer dragging a leg, after 150 or 200 yards I still hadn't found a drop of blood. Apparently Ken was right – I had missed again.

I had to confirm this to everyone when Ken's voice came over the radio to ask whether I had found a blood trail. "No," I seethed. "There's nothing." I wanted desperately to unleash a stream of obscenities that would make Happy Gilmore sound like Gandhi.

"That's OK," Ken said with his customary chuckle, "That's just not your role. We'll find out what your role is, but you're just not the guy who puts meat on the pole." I'm not sure if he intended that remark to encourage me, but it didn't.

There was nothing else to do but continue the drive. Then, just as I was straining to put all the black thoughts out of my head, a deer seemed to pop up out of the ground. It was about 50 yards to my left, directly in front of Bartell. "Phil, there's a deer!" I said quickly as I snapped my rifle up and scanned the woods. "Do you see it?"

"I did, but I can't see it now," came his reply. Indeed, the deer seemed to dematerialize as quickly as it arrived in the first place. We took a few cautious steps forward.

Instantly, the saplings in front of Bartell came alive and he fired a shot with the muzzleloader. The deer picked up speed and blurred by me in two jumps, screened by thick brush.

Once again, I helplessly watched a running deer storm away from me. "There's one coming right in front of you, Mark!" I hollered to Heider, who didn't have an antlerless license. "Yell up to Andy to get ready."

"Andy," he complied, "Get ready, there's one coming!"

And then something amazing happened.

At Heider's yell, the doe stopped in her tracks. It was the last mistake of her life.

She was perhaps 50 yards to my right front, standing perfectly still and nearly broadside to me. Only one thought went through my head: Finally!

There was still a tangle of branches between us, but then that's why we carry brush guns on the Allegheny, isn't it? I might miss running shots all day long, but I wasn't going to miss one like this. I glued the crosshairs to a spot just behind her shoulder and fired without hesitating.

The doe shuddered once then stood perfectly still. I levered another round into the chamber, but when I saw her take an unsteady step forward I knew I wouldn't need it. She was dead on her feet.

"Yeah!" I hollered in a celebration of joy and relief. "I got her!"

"No, she's still walking here in front of me," said Heider.

"Don't worry about it," I said, suddenly cocky at my newfound success. "She's dead."

"You sure?" he asked uncertainly. Then, as she staggered forward another few steps, he added, "Oh, yeah. I see her now. She's done. That's a lung shot."

"Yep," I said gleefully. At that second, as though the impact of that single syllable was more than she could bear, the doe toppled.

We walked over to examine the downed whitetail, which turned out to be a year and a half old doe weighing 100 pounds. After the agony of the previous 24 hours – in fact, of the entire fall to that point – I was as proud and thrilled as the day I shot my biggest buck.

When I rolled her onto her back, I noticed a bullet hole in her left rear leg. "Hey, look here, Phil," I said in to Bartell, who had walked over to join in the post-shot celebration. "It looks like you hit her after all."

"That wasn't from me," he insisted. The unfamiliar set trigger on his flintlock had caused the gun to go off well before he was ready. He was sure he hadn't hit the deer at all.

"I guess you hit it back on the other side of the road after all," said Heider. "I told you it was dragging that back leg," he added cheerfully.

I looked closer at the hole on the inside of her thigh. For whatever reason, not a single drop of blood had dripped out of the hole onto the white fur around it. Somehow the bullet had passed through her leg without causing it to bleed, though she dragged the leg as she ran. Eventually, she must have stopped to rest it, where Bartell and I stumbled onto her again.

With the drive still going on, I let the others move ahead while I prepared to gut the doe. I leaned my gun against a tree, peeled off my coat, and pulled my knife from its sheath. The knife, a gift from Pam shortly after we got married, had accompanied me on every big game hunt since then.

As that thought came to me, I let it tow me into a reverie on deer hunting, and on this deer in particular. This was my first season of deer hunting on public land in more than a decade, and it had posed more of a challenge than I initially supposed. This was also my first deer on the Allegheny National Forest, a place that has a special home in my soul – and, as I had found this fall, the souls of so many others.

In the true tradition of a Pennsylvania hunter, a success in deer season was more than enough to wash away the failures of earlier outings. Here, especially on the Allegheny, it's deer season that counts.

On top of everything else, I thought as I grinned to myself, I did my civic duty. The deer had been shot north of Kinzua Creek, putting it within the boundaries of the KQDC. My smile widened as I realized I would have a doe to record at deCallesta's check station at the Westline Inn. And I would get two raffle tickets to boot!

I had just finished gutting the doe when Ken, fulfilling his duties as camp captain, came back to check on me. His jack-o-lantern grin may have been broader than mine.

"You did it, buddy," he said. "You finally got one to fall. Nice job."

"I finally got one to stand still," I said emphatically.

I recounted the shot for Ken, pointing out the deer's route and its last, fatal choice to stop in the brush.

"Bad decision," he agreed.

We roped the doe and dragged her uphill to the road. By the time we got there, the rest of the group was waiting there to pick us up and transport us back to my truck.

I recounted the story once more and accepted their congratulations. "See," said Novosel, turning to Ken. "You shouldn't have challenged him."

"What?" said Ken, momentarily confused.

"You told him on the radio that it wasn't his job to get a deer and five minutes later he shot one," he said with a hearty chuckle. "I think you pissed him off so he had to show you up."

"That's right!" I chimed in, laughing. "Don't ever challenge me."

By the time we reached my truck, it was nearly midday and the entire group had to call it quits. Many of them would be back on Saturday to try again to fill their tags. But for the opening of the 2004 season, mine would be the last deer taken out of Camp Stockert.

We went back to camp and packed to leave. First, though, we gathered around the meat pole for a series of photos and a few more rounds of laughter. It was the traditional victory ritual of a successful hunting camp and judging from the framed photos hanging on the walls of Camp Stockert, it has been going on here for generations.

Although the tempting aroma of another Novosel meal drifted through the camp's open door, I had to hurry off to the check station, so I declined lunch. I said my goodbyes and thanked everyone in camp then backed the Ford out onto the road.

As I pulled out, I thought of the lows of yesterday's hunt – the throng of hunters surrounding me in the morning, the miss in the creek – and the soaring feeling that I still had from this morning's hunt. My chest swelled as I breathed the mountain air deep into my lungs.

I punched the radio on and let the music pump through the speakers ("I hope you like country music," Ken had told me on my first trip to Camp Stockert, "because that's all we get up here.").

Country star Darryl Worley was singing his hit song *Awful Beautiful Life*:

I laid in bed that night and thought about the day, and how my life is like a roller coaster ride,
The ups and downs and crazy turns along the way, it'll throw you off if you don't hold on tight.

I turned the volume up as high as it would go.

CHAPTER 10

WILDERNESS ON THE WATER

Christmas 2004 was one of the most joyful of my adult life. For starters, there were my kids. At ages 11, 8, and 5, respectively, Rachel, Stephanie, and Jake were all in the prime period of Santa enjoyment and their enthusiasm was contagious. We also had the predictably pleasant visits with my parents, and my sisters and their families.

But this year, for the first time in over a decade, we were also able to spend the holiday season with my in-laws. Pam's mom, Lynn, had recently retired so both Lynn and Pam's dad, Gene, made the trip from Florida to stay with us. Unlike a stereotypical son-in-law, I love Pam's parents dearly and their visit brought yet another dimension to the warmth of our holiday hearth. To top things off, we were grilling the world's most delicious sausage for breakfast each morning – made from my Allegheny National Forest deer.

The slight downside to my wonderful life was that I couldn't free up any time for hunting between deer season and Christmas. Still, as I sat in front of the fire on Christmas morning, surrounded by our rotund Christmas tree, heaps of gift boxes and wrapping paper, and our laughing, squealing, shouting family, I was positive it was a trade I would make every time. Besides, I knew my time on the Allegheny was coming again.

While checking in for a deer season update, I had wrangled an invitation from Dan Brophy for an Allegheny River duck and goose hunt. This time there would be no fooling with turkeys or splitting time between the woods and the river. We were going waterfowling all the way, which was exactly to Dan's liking.

I had also unabashedly invited myself along on a snowshoe hare hunt with the Forest Service's Mary Hosmer, the day after my waterfowling date. It would be two days of shotgunning on the Allegheny, but for species – and in habitats – that could hardly be more different.

Unlike my early season goose hunts at Buzzard Swamp, I wasn't taking Hunter along on this trip. Although he's hunted several times for late season grouse in subzero temperatures, his short coat just wouldn't give him enough protection in the icy waters of December. He was clearly chagrined at this decision when I ordered him back into the house after loading the pickup in the predawn hours of the 28th.

"Maybe Mom will give you a piece of deer sausage when she gets up," I whispered to him as I closed the door on his gray muzzle.

Although we had only a dusting of snow on the ground now, temperatures had plummeted since deer season. As I rolled through the inky night an electronic bank sign pierced the darkness, shouting that it was 4:48 AM and 9 degrees Fahrenheit. I grimaced; both numbers were too low for my comfort.

As planned, I met Dan at his house, about 45 minutes southwest of the Allegheny National Forest. The aluminum johnboat was already loaded when I pulled in the driveway. I helped him toss in the decoys and we were on our way.

We made a quick stop at Camp Brophy then headed back upriver. Our strategy for the morning was to set mallard and goose decoys in the river just below the mouth of Hickory Creek, on the west bank of the Allegheny River. If things slowed down over the dekes, we could drop the johnboat in river and float downstream.

The morning's set-up was just a few dozen yards above the northern tip of Kings Island, one of seven islands in the Allegheny River Islands Wilderness. This riverine archipelago begins with Crull's Island, near the Beanfield, and extends south for about 15 miles along the river. Besides Crull's (96 acres) and Kings (36 acres), the other islands within the Wilderness are Thompson's (67 acres), Baker (also 67 acres, and the site of my first duck hunting expedition with Dan), Courson (62 acres), R. Thompson's (30 acres), and No-Name (10 acres).

At just 362 acres, the Allegheny River Islands Wilderness is one of the smallest Wilderness Areas designated since the Wilderness Act was first passed in 1964 (Pelican Island, Florida, is the tiniest at just 5 acres). The River Islands were designated by Congress in 1984, becoming – along with the Allegheny's Hickory Creek Wilderness – another link in the 106 million-acre Wilderness network that stretches across the American landscape. While not as vast as Alaska's 8 million-acre Arctic Wilderness Area or as pristine as Wyoming's Teton Wilderness, the Allegheny River Islands have one distinction that sets them apart from every other federal Wilderness: they served as inspiration for the Wilderness Act itself.

In June 1937, 31-year old Howard Zahniser and his wife Alice decided to take a canoe trip down the Allegheny River from Olean, New York to their home in the Allegheny National Forest town of Tionesta. Zahniser's journal from that trip shows his special affinity for the stretch of river above his hometown: "We paddled on, finding the islands interesting. It was a clear blue June day...As we went under the bridge at West Hickory after winding through the islands, we saw two eagles flying high over...The canoeing from Hickory on had the added interest of the faint recollection of familiar things." [43]

At the time of his Allegheny River journey, Zahniser was working for the forerunner agency of the US Fish and Wildlife Service. He later worked for both the USDA and the National Park Service. In 1945, however, Zahniser left the employ of the federal government to become the executive secretary of the Wilderness Society.

At the head of this environmental activist group, Zahniser became the torchbearer for Congressional Wilderness designations, calling for "a concerted effort for a positive program that will establish an enduring system of areas where we can be at peace and not forever feel that the wilderness is a battleground."[44] But when a 1946 proposal for a "Federal Wildlands Project" fell flat, Zahniser realized a stronger approach would be needed. Within the next decade he started a grassroots campaign to rally the public to his cause while simultaneously working over members of Congress at every opportunity. Zahniser's pursuit was so zealous that he enlisted his four young children to pass out pamphlets on the steps of the Capital.

He was so consumed with the needs of his monumental task that he convinced a Georgetown tailor "to make him suits whose coats featured four supersized inside pockets. These became veritable fabric filing cabinets that usually held wilderness bill propaganda, Wilderness Society membership information and applications, a book by Thoreau, and another book by either Dante or Blake."[45]

The Wilderness Act was finally signed into law by President Lyndon Johnson on September 3, 1964. Howard Zahniser, tragically, never lived to see that historic moment.

"He'd just go and go, often 30 hours at a stretch," Alice said later, "In the end he just spent himself out."[46] He died on May 5, 1964, two days after testifying at the final congressional hearing on the Wilderness Act.

On August 13, 2001, the man who became the Moses of his cause – leading his followers into the Wilderness rather than out of it – was honored by the dedication of a historical marker near his hometown of Tionesta. To me it seems ironic: the person who spent his life attempting to create an escape from the constructs of mankind being memorialized by a metal sign adjacent to Route 62.

Still, the memorial sign overlooks part of the Allegheny River Wilderness Islands and they have their own tales to tell. In fact, they're a microcosm of human activity on the Allegheny National Forest itself. The river corridor was heavily used by Eastern Woodland Indians, the islands were logged during the pioneer era, Crull's Island was once farmed as part of the Irvine plantation, and Kings Island has two abandoned oil wells. Even the military has gotten involved – in August 1779, Thompson's Island was the site of the only Revolutionary War battle fought in northwestern Pennsylvania.

On this December morning, 226 years later, the only shooting along the Allegheny River would come not from a musket, but from Dan's Mossberg 835 and my Crescent side by side, which, admittedly, appears old enough to have been used in the Revolution. Unlike our last time together on the river, when a fishing tournament put an early end to our waterfowling, it seemed like the bitter cold weather had kept the less hardy – or perhaps, more sensible – folks at home.

As we cracked through the ice along the edge of the river to set our spread of Canada goose and mallard decoys, the only other sign of human life were occasional passing headlights on Route 62 across the river. Our set-up was just a mile or so north of Zahniser's hometown of Tionesta and smack in the middle of the Allegheny River Wilderness Islands.

Given the 15-degree temperature at daybreak and the thick layer of ice along the bank, it took us a little longer to get set up than we wanted. As a result, a flock of geese winged upriver from their overnight roost before we even loaded our guns. It was a discouraging start, made worse when the same thing happened a few minutes later from upriver – a second flock of geese had spent the night in the eddy at the mouth of Hickory Creek.

"Dang it!" Dan complained. "I wanted to check out both of those spots once we had the decoys set! We should have just gone there first. We both could have had a couple of birds out of those flocks."

We had little time to dwell on the problem, though, because a pair of mergansers distracted us by buzzing upriver past our half-finished spread.

"Man, the birds are flying today," said Dan, recovering his enthusiasm. "Let's get these dekes out and quit messing around."

We took up spots on either side of the twin trunks of a massive silver maple tree. The ice wasn't thick enough to support us for long, so our waders were soon immersed in a foot of chilling water.

Dan was properly outfitted for the occasion in snow camo coveralls, which blended perfectly with the white-gray of our natural blind. I, on the other hand, covered my red and black Woolrich coat with a white blanket. With the cover draped over me and pulled tight around my chin, I felt like an overgrown Little White Riding Hood. It was embarrassing...until the next duck flew directly at me.

As the bufflehead winged upriver, the branches of the trees beside us screened it until it almost passed our spread. At that point he spied our decoys, executed a ninety-degree turn in our direction and zoomed in before Dan even had a chance to call.

The buff's flight line made it appear that he was going to crash directly into my chest. Waiting until the bird was within range, Dan gave me the call to "Take him!"

I clumsily tossed off the blanket, drew the old double to my shoulder and fired. And missed. Then fired again. And missed.

It was good old-fashioned lousy shooting, but we didn't have time to mope. This time it was two mergansers that zipped like white and black missiles up the river.

Dan and I both opened up as the birds flew by our spread. Like many of the shots we would end up with that day, these were long ones, 30 yards at least, and we both missed.

As the mergansers disappeared upstream, Dan explained that wary birds are a fact of life when hunting the late season on the Allegheny River. "There's just so much hunting pressure all season long that they get pretty spooked," he said in a matter-of-fact tone. "You just have to get used to having all long, fast shots."

A few minutes later, a bald eagle sailed overhead, reminding me of Zahniser's journal entry. Its graceful flight also made me think of the eagles we had seen on the Clarion River in the early duck season, which jogged my memory that this stretch of the Allegheny River, like the Clarion, has Wild and Scenic designation. The sight of an eagle now seems permanently associated with the phrase "Wild and Scenic" in my mind.

Shortly after the eagle glided over, we had another chance at a duck. This time I let the expert handle the chore.

In fact, I had no choice because the tree branches once again blocked my view. The first indication I had that the hen mallard was in the vicinity was the soft splash she made when she settled into our decoy spread. Carefully craning my neck to find the source of the sound, I heard Dan whisper, "Go ahead, shoot it."

Before I could answer I heard another splash from the river followed by a roar from Dan's Mossberg. I finally caught a glimpse of the duck as it flopped into the icy black river.

We scrambled onto the ice as Dan sent nine-month old Cassie into the frigid water to bring back the bird. It wasn't the cold morning or the freezing water around my feet that sent a quick chill down my backbone as the Lab pup swam out and nabbed the still-thrashing bird. The retrieve was truly a thing of beauty.

"Did you hear me whispering to you to take it?" Dan asked as Cassie covered the last few yards.

"Yeah, I heard you," I answered, "but I couldn't see it."

"I didn't know why you weren't shooting," he replied, "but it started to fly off, so I just took it."

"I'm glad you did," I said. "I'd have never even gotten a shot at it."

Cassie deposited the bird at Dan's feet to a chorus of "Good girl!" from both of us. When she shook the river water from her coat, I could hear the clinking of ice pellets flying off.

We settled back into our natural blind and I nestled back under my blanket. Dan called for a bit, but the calls soon froze so we simply sat and waited for ducks to come in.

And come in they did. Over the next hour or so, we blasted at nearly a dozen more birds – mostly mergansers at 40 to 50 yards – without success.

The long distance shots were the main factor in our misses. I fired at one merganser flying inches off the water, and then watched it sail on downriver.

"How in the hell did I miss that bird?" I griped. "I was right on it!"

"You didn't," laughed Dan. "You strafed it. I saw your pattern hit the water – it hit on both sides of the bird. He was just too far out to bring him down."

The extreme cold also caused us problems. Besides Dan's frozen duck calls, I missed a chance at a drake mallard that was coasting in to the decoy spread because the glove on my trigger hand froze to the metal on the side of the shotgun.

When a few too many birds had snuck in on us, we decided to move upriver a few paces to a spot that had slightly less tree cover. This didn't seem to bother the ducks any, as they continued to fly by in singles and pairs every ten minutes or so.

In between arrivals, Dan and I conversed in hushed tones. Like virtually everyone else in western Pennsylvania at this point, we talked about the impressive season of the 12-1 Pittsburgh Steelers. At one point, I mentioned a video clip I had recently seen in which a soldier in Iraq asked Secretary of Defense Donald Rumsfeld whether the soldiers would be able to get satellite TV, "so that we can watch the Steelers win the Super Bowl." I chuckled as I recounted the story to Dan, telling him how the entire crowd of soldiers had erupted in cheers. Being both a Steeler fan and a volunteer soldier, I figured he would get a kick out of the story.

"Those must have been PA National Guard," Dan said, more quietly than I expected.

"I don't know for sure," I replied, a little taken aback by the gravity in his tone.

"That sounds like my boys in the National Guard," he said. He wasn't laughing.

"Did you hear about the soldier from West Virginia that got killed in the mess hall bombing?" he asked after a moment.[47] I allowed that I had.

"He was apparently a big Steeler fan," said Dan. "I heard a news report where they said he was going to be coming home soon and his family was going to get Steeler tickets for him. That was the only thing he wanted to do when he got home."

In the silence that followed, I began to realize what a strain it was for Dan to be here on the Allegheny enjoying the sport he loves while his fellow Guardsmen dealt with a faceless menace each day on the other side of the planet. Stuck at a rare loss for words, I was thankful for the distraction when the next duck came along.

We had sporadic shooting all morning, but by 10:30 it tapered off so we decided to move on to the amphibious phase of our hunt. The idea was to cross the West Hickory Bridge then put the johnboat in at the public boat launch on the east side of the river. When we got halfway across the one-lane bridge, however, we saw that this was going to be impossible. The launch was already occupied – by a flock of more than 50 geese.

This was the ultimate good news/bad news scenario. The good news was that the geese we were looking for were now milling about lazily just a few yards below us. The bad news was that we had no way to get at them; if we drove into the boat launch parking lot they would unquestionably be gone as soon as we opened the truck doors.

The next closest public launch that either of us knew of was at Buckaloons, much too far upstream. We had to find a place to put in upriver, but not too far upriver, of the West Hickory Bridge. Suddenly Dan had an idea.

"There's a place about a half-mile up from here," he said quickly. "My dad knows the people who own it. The bank's normally too steep to get in and out, but with the water up we can probably make it OK. And I think I can leave my truck there without any problem. I just hope it's not locked."

"Well, let's go," I said without hesitation. "Those geese are just standing there waiting for us."

Luckily, the gate on the driveway was open and we were able to drive to the river's edge. The river was plenty high enough to get the johnboat in safely, so we locked Dan's truck ("If it gets towed, it gets towed," he said as we walked away.) and shoved the boat out into the river.

The going was a little dicey at first, as the swift, swirling current tried repeatedly to shove us into the overhanging brush along the riverbank. I eyed the cold, dark water with trepidation. My mishap on the Clarion in early October had been chilly but laughable; a dip in the rushing Allegheny in December could easily be deadly. Soon, however, we got our navigation under control and glided silently downstream.

By this time, the geese were within sight, ambling casually on the bank and in the parking lot of the boat launch. As we floated nearer, they crept toward the water's edge.

The only safe shooting direction was directly downriver. This meant we would need to drift within range of the geese, and then somehow flush them into the air. At that point, we would just have to hope they flew downstream.

We were still about 50 or so yards away from the birds, which were now clustered along the bank and poised to fly, when the problem of flushing them was solved for us. A worker at the maintenance building behind the boat launch slammed his truck door and the geese launched into the air as if they had been jolted.

Dan and I both opened up on the retreating flock, emptying our guns at them as they winged off downriver. I thought I saw one dip a little at my second shot and Dan thought he had hit one too, but the range was just too far and no birds fell. The timing of the flush had been just a bit too soon – in another few seconds we would have been within easy killing distance.

Still, it was an exciting moment. And, as Dan pointed out, we were floating the same direction the geese were flying. There was a good chance we would see them again.

We drifted quickly on the fast-flowing river and after we passed West Hickory, we rowed over toward the west bank. Dan knew the area well enough to realize where we could and could not shoot due to the camps and houses near the shore.

Just below West Hickory we spied a merganser sitting among a tangle of tree branches along the west bank. Dan tried to work the boat in closer as he told me, "If he starts to fly, shoot."

Instantly, the bird took off and I shot, even though we were probably out of range. "No sense taking extra shells home," I joked lamely.

"That's right," agreed Dan reassuringly. "You can't hit 'em if you don't shoot."

Although I was trying to laugh off the misses, I told Dan that I was really disappointed that I hadn't shot a duck this morning. After all, I had never gotten one.

"Really?" he asked in amazement.

"Yeah," I replied. "I've only been duck hunting twice before today and I didn't get anything either time. I've shot a few geese, but never a duck."

"Well, don't worry," he assured me. "We'll get you a duck today."

We soon passed the mouth of Hickory Creek and crouched in readiness as we reached our decoy spread, which was still bobbing on the river. There were no live birds in it, though, so we drifted on by.

Dan steered the boat into the channel on the west side of Kings Island and as we rounded a bend, we saw a flock of Canadas lifting off the water 100 yards downstream. There looked to be at least 100 geese, with a few ducks mixed in as well. Both Dan and I were now confident that we would get more shooting before the day was over.

We were now just a short distance above the mouth of Dawson Run, approaching the northern tip of Baker Island. Dan, stretching his neck to peek above a berm along the river's edge, suddenly jerked down like a turtle retreating into its shell.

"There's a flock of geese," he whispered hurriedly. "They're on the bank right up around the bend. Get ready."

Dan pulled the oars into the johnboat and forced Cassie to lie down. Guns at the ready, we both hunkered down to the gunwales, trying to make our profile as tiny as possible.

The current of Dawson Run shoved the boat around the bend and as we rounded the point, there stood a flock of a dozen geese, just 40 yards away.

Amazingly, they seemed to ignore our presence as we floated nearer – 35 yards, 30, 25. Still bent with my chin to my knees, I pulled the double gun to my chest and tensed for Dan's "Take 'em" call.

The geese now sensed trouble and started moving to the water's edge in preparation for flight. "Wa-a-a-it," Dan whispered, seemingly as much to himself as to me. "Hold on."

Suddenly, about 15 yards from the bow of the boat, a duck popped to the surface. Shocked at its sudden appearance I glanced back at Dan for instructions.

"Do you see that duck?" I asked, barely able to keep my voice to a whisper.

"Yeah," he said. "When they go, you shoot the geese and I'll take the duck."

"What?" I croaked hoarsely. "Why don't you take the geese and I'll take the duck?"

Dan looked at me quizzically and I searched for a diplomatic – and quick – way to remind him that I'd never taken a duck. Luckily, he remembered on his own and the discussion ended before we floated completely past the birds.

"Oh, yeah, that's right," he said with a shake of his head. "What am I thinking? You shoot the duck."

"OK," I said, turning back to face the birds and snickering under my breath at the absurdity of the debate.

A split second later, chaos erupted.

The little bird suddenly realized its precarious position in relation to our boat and started churning for the sky. I fired and splashed it back into the dark water.

My shot immediately set off the geese. As they erupted off the water, Dan knocked one back down and it flapped to the bank.

I swung the antique Crescent toward the rest of the geese, intent on taking one with my second shot. But I was momentarily distracted by the flapping duck in front of me – I didn't want my first-ever duck getting away – and when I turned my attention back to the Canadas, they were already out of range.

With two birds down, one in the water and one on the bank, Cassie was only too happy to get in the water. Within seconds, she nabbed the duck and brought it up to the side of the boat. That was when our serious waterfowling trip devolved into comedy.

Cassie swam the bird up to the downstream side of the boat, which meant that the river was pushing it against her. As the aluminum hull repeatedly clunked against her shoulder, she managed to position herself at the exact spot where neither Dan nor I could get a handhold to pull her back in.

Finally, with nothing else to use as a handle, I tried to grab the duck that was still dangling from her mouth and use it to lug her toward me. Cassie, well-trained retriever that she is, took this as a signal to release the bird. She did, and, instead of grasping a 60-pound dog, I found myself holding only a 60-ounce duck.

By now, both Dan and I were giggling like a couple of 10-year old girls at a slumber party. Still struggling to get Cassie aboard, I gave her a push on the head, forcing her back toward Dan. Using her tail as a tow rope, he pulled her backward.

Then, to my surprise, Dan said quickly, "That goose isn't dead yet. It's moving around. You keep an eye on it and I'll get her in the boat."

Sure enough, when I looked toward the bank, the bird that I thought was long dead was walking around like he couldn't figure out why his friends had left in such a hurry. Not wanting to fill the bird with any more steel shot than was necessary, I waited, covering him with my shotgun like Barney Fife arresting one of America's Most Wanted.

I could hear Dan and Cassie flopping around behind me, but I didn't want to look away from the goose, which was now strolling toward the river's edge. I wasn't sure whether it could take off, but it appeared to want to.

"Dan, this bird's headed toward the water."

"OK," Dan grunted. "Just keep it covered."

The goose cocked its wings. "Uh, Dan," I said uncertainly.

He looked up from his struggles with Cassie. "Oh, man!" he said hurriedly, "Shoot it, quick!"

He didn't have to tell me twice. I lined up the beads on its head and at the report of the gun, the big bird collapsed in a heap about five feet from the river's edge.

With both birds now safely out of commission, we both turned our attention to Cassie and wrestled her aboard. Once she was in, we took a second to congratulate each other.

"That was awesome, wasn't it?" gushed Dan. "It was bizarre the way that duck just appeared."

"That," I agreed with a cheek-splitting grin, "was about as strange a double as you're ever going to get."

Then I turned back toward where the goose had fallen. "Oh, crap."

Somehow, the twice-killed Canada had dragged itself into the river and was now floating off downstream. We could still recover him, but now it was going to take ten times longer and mess up the rest of our hunt. It was as if, in a final defiant act, the goose was flipping us a figurative middle finger: our bird was giving us the bird. I couldn't help but shake my head in wonder and appreciation.

With Dan rowing for all he was worth, we eventually caught up with the drifting goose. After retrieving it we floated the last few hundred yards to Camp Brophy without firing another shot. We did see a few more ducks and geese in that stretch, but they were much too far away.

Once on shore, Dan asked to examine my little brown duck more closely. He turned it over carefully then said slowly, "I'm pretty sure this is a Fulvous Tree Duck. These are really unusual up here."

Not catching the significance at first, all I said was, "Really?"

"Yeah," he replied. "They're rare enough that the limit is just one bird."

A quick check of a Camp Brophy field guide confirmed Dan's identification. "That's awesome!" he exclaimed. "You shot your limit on your first bird! I can't believe you shot one of those for your first duck. You should be psyched."

I was psyched, but we still had work to do. After posing for some pictures with our mixed bag, we stowed the boat and hung our wet gear, then drove back to pick up the decoys. As we walked out toward our set, a mallard flushed off the water just downriver and another pair flew by. Dan and I wheeled and sprinted back to the truck for our guns.

As we stalked back toward the river, Dan said, "I wonder if any landed in our decoys while we were gone?" As if on cue, a merganser burst off the water and made for the middle of the river.

I pulled up first. My shot appeared to wing the bird slightly, but Dan's two follow-ups had no effect and the bird escaped. It was perhaps the most fitting end possible to our day on the Allegheny River.

As a postscript to our hunt, Dan told me later that he squeezed in one more waterfowl hunt last winter, about a month after our day on the water. Once again, he was floating the Allegheny River for geese, this time with three friends who had never been waterfowling before.

"We were coming around the corner at Dawson Run, where you and I shot those birds," Dan told me. "And there were about 50 geese right there, about 10 yards away from us." His voice rose in excitement at the memory.

"We laid into them," he said with a laugh. "We shot seven between the four of us. Six of them had bands!"

Dan collected two of the banded birds and when he called them in, he got a pleasant surprise. "Two of those bands had $100 rewards on them!" he said. "We split the reward four ways, but I told them, 'Guys, don't think it's like this every time. This will never happen again.'"

Even without banded birds or rewards, I thought our December hunt was a tremendous success and I was thrilled with my prize. It was late in the day by the time Dan and I got back to camp and stowed the remainder of the gear. Dan had to leave so I thanked him for the 37th time for helping me get my first duck.

"It's funny," he said as we stood in the driveway, "You come home muddy and wet and cold and carrying all this stuff, and all you have to show when someone says 'Did you get anything?' is this one little bird. People look at you like you're nuts."

"But it's worth it for that one little bird," I said with a grin.

"To you and me, sure. But not to people who don't understand," he finished.

I understood.

With an hour left before sundown, I decided to take the Pennsylvania rifle out for the rest of the day. In Pennsylvania, muzzleloader season comes back in immediately after Christmas ("It doesn't come in on Christmas Day," Pam often reminds me, "because they want to keep the divorce rate down."). I elected to hunt near the spot where Dan had taken his turkey back in the fall.

I settled myself against a stump, looking out over the hemlocks and grapevines. For an hour and a half I sat, peacefully reflecting on the day's excitement and on the pleasurable days that had preceded it. I didn't see even a hint of a deer...and I didn't care a bit.

Eventually, the sun glided over the ridge behind me. It was as though a stopper had been pulled and the color drained out of the day.

Though it was turning bitterly cold again and I was weary through every bone, I hated to leave, to admit that this glorious day was over. Days of enjoyment with good friends are far too few. I wanted to cling to every second of this one.

CHAPTER 11

SNOWSHOEING

Maybe it was because I had left a houseful of people at home. Or maybe it was because I just didn't want this day to end, even after sundown. Whatever the reason, I didn't feel like eating by myself at Camp Brophy, so I drove over to the Hickory Nut Inn for dinner.

Although the sign outside the Hickory Nut says "Family Restaurant," the interior looks suspiciously like a bar. That, in fact, was what I liked about it.

The chalkboard dangling precariously above rows of dusty liquor bottles proclaimed that tonight was "Wing Night" with "50 cent wings all night." When I asked the twenty-something bartender how much the wings were normally, she looked blankly at me for a second or two before answering, "Fifty cents."

The bar was still glowing with leftover Christmas decorations and a handwritten sign thumbtacked to the wall announced next weekend's New Year's party. The bartender told me her name was Holly and she seemed to know everyone's name in the place except mine.

I listened to the half-shouted conversations from the dozen men and women clustered around the bar. Like Dan and I earlier, they mostly discussed whether the Steelers would beat the Buffalo Bills on Sunday. There were in-depth analyses of the team's playoff prospects and the odds of reaching the Super Bowl. It was at least as entertaining, if about one-tenth as accurate, as anything on ESPN.

One patron, after fiddling for several minutes with his cell phone, got up to use the payphone instead. "This might be the only county in the state where people still use payphones," announced another man, "They just built a new cell tower up on German Hill and there's still no damn cell service up here."

"It's because of the trees," yet another bar dweller chimed in.

It was a strong test of my personal restraint in not asking for further explanation of that theory.

A day on the frigid river had made me hungrier than I realized so I chased my bowl of beef stew with a ham sandwich and fries. Even with that and a celebratory beer, fifteen bucks covered the meal and still left Holly a decent tip.

When I got back to Camp Brophy, I could see my breath – while standing in the kitchen. I quickly built a fire in the woodstove, which was the sole source of heat. This worked a little, but I still opted to sleep on the couch in front of the wood stove rather than risking frostbite in the back bedroom.

The fire burned out well before morning and the last lingering warmth from the stove did little to entice me out of my sleeping bag when the alarm chimed. Finally, after a few stolen minutes of half-slumber, I grudgingly rolled off the couch and into the day.

After cleaning up and loading the truck, I followed Camp Brophy custom by wadding up newspaper and putting kindling in the wood stove so that the next person could simply ignite it with the touch of a match. When the last piece of wood was added, I was out the door and off to Marienville to meet Mary Hosmer for our snowshoe hare hunt.

I was supposed to meet Mary at the Uni-Mart in Marienville at 9 AM. I arrived early, but by that time I needed to find a restroom. I knew from experience that the Uni-Mart didn't have one, so I headed a couple of miles further east to use the outhouse at Buzzard Swamp.

When I pulled in, there were two empty trucks in the lot. When I returned from the restroom another car had joined them. When I saw a group piling out of the car in hunter orange clothing I decided to stop to chat.

"What are you guys out for?" I asked, just as their beagle sprung from the backseat of the car, "Snowshoes?"

The four men declared that they were after birds, rabbits, hares, anything they could get. It turned out that they were in the area visiting friends and had decided at the last moment to squeeze in a morning hunt. The group was from Ft. Lauderdale, Florida.

"Good for you," I said, although they already looked uncomfortable in the frigid air. Then, bending down to pet their dog, I asked, "Is he a pretty good hunter?" This brought a chorus of laughter.

"Nah," one of them said. "He's a city dog. We just decided we'd bring him out here today and let him have a run. We want to see what he can do."

I wished them luck and headed back into town. When I got back to the Uni-Mart, Mary and her friends still weren't there, so I went inside to pick up some breakfast. I smiled to myself when another store customer, after spying my brush pants, flannel shirt, and orange cap, discreetly turned to the clerk and asked, "Deer season isn't still in, is it?"

A master of the obvious, the teenaged clerk said that he didn't know what season was in now, but pointed at me and said, "He might know."

The customer, an older gentleman, sheepishly turned toward me and started to ask again, but I decided to save him a little embarrassment by answering first. "There's a little bit of everything in now," I said. "It's muzzleloader season for deer. That's what most people are probably after now. I'm hunting for snowshoe hares today, and yesterday I was duck hunting. Like I said, it's a mix of things right now."

"Oh, I see," he said reacting kindly to my informative attitude. "I was just curious." And then, as he turned to walk out of the store, he briefly turned back and added, "Good luck."

"Thanks," I replied with a wave. "Have a happy New Year."

I felt good about the encounter and the chance to briefly become an ambassador for the hunting community. A few minutes later, Hosmer, a true ambassador for the hunting community, pulled into the parking lot in her pickup.

Actually, Mary is less like an ambassador for hunting and more like its publicity department. To say she wears her passion for hunting on her sleeve, though, would be incorrect. She wears it on her truck.

By my count, Mary's pickup had at least a dozen stickers, magnets, and decals advertising her hunting and conservation affiliations. The largest of these was the Ruffed Grouse Society 'Sponsor' sign that took up most of her driver's side door, but the National Wild Turkey Federation, Ducks Unlimited, and Pheasants Forever also had prominent billing on the fenders and tailgate.

Mary says these groups first popped up on her personal radar when she was a biologist with the USFWS. "Some of those groups just stand out," she says earnestly. "I really bought into what they were doing."

She feels that the participation of hunter-based conservation groups is stronger on the Allegheny than the other National Forests in which she has worked. "The interest has been high everywhere," she says, "but I'd have to say that it's higher here."

Perhaps that's one reason that, after 10 years of bouncing from one National Forest to another, she has spent the last 15 here. For Mary, a native of Michigan's Upper Peninsula, a strong hunter-conservation community must seem like home.

"When I was about 12 years old," she told me, "Dad took me snowshoeing out in the Dolly Lake Wilderness. He took me all the way back into the Wilderness – it was a long way for a little girl to go on snowshoes – but he kept going. He took me back into some pines and showed me some lynx tracks. Dad was a trapper so he knew where they were. He said, 'I want you to look at these, Mary. These are lynx tracks and this is the last one. The other trappers are in here now and they're going to catch this one, then they will all be gone.' I can really appreciate now how important that was."

Another lasting lesson from Mary's youth was also advertised on the tailgate of her truck, spelled out in black lettering on a stark white background. In large capital letters, the sticker said simply, "BEAGLER."

"When we kids were little, Dad had to get all of us out of the house. So we hunted," she says in a matter of fact tone.

"From the first of October through the first of April, we were either hunting or ice fishing." Her absolute favorite, though, was hunting snowshoe hares among the cedars of the UP.

"We always had beagles to hunt snowshoe hare. We ate a lot of hasenpfeffer from all the snowshoe hare we shot," she says with a laugh. "I don't believe that I ate cow until I was 15 or 16 years old."

When she came to the Allegheny, Hosmer rediscovered her love for hares – and beagles. "I had a Springer Spaniel to hunt ruffed grouse when I moved here," she recalls. "My Springer Spaniel was ancient, so I started looking around for a new dog and I found a beagle club down the road." You can guess how it goes from there.

When asked how many beagles she owns today, Mary says, "I'm actually down right now. I have five." Then she gushes, "I love it, I absolutely love it. It's a throwback to when I was a kid, when Dad used to let the beagles sleep in the bed with us."

Like most of us, Mary would hunt seven days a week if she could. She spends most of her time chasing ruffed grouse, but during Pennsylvania's one week snowshoe hare season (always the week between Christmas and New Year's) she is out after hares in every spare minute.

"I only harvest one a year. That's my personal limit," she explains. "But I've been able to take that one every year except two out of the past ten."

"Probably the best fun I ever had," Hosmer continues, "was a little short hunt, just west of Ridgway. The Forest Service had done some non-commercial tree harvest there in cooperation with the Ruffed Grouse Society. I took a group of three young people with me who had never shot snowshoe hare before.

"My beagle, Trouble, went in the bottom of a log pile and the snowshoe hare squirted out the top. It ran right past one of the kids, but he never shot. I asked him why he didn't shoot and he said, 'Shoot?! That thing was a gray ghost!' But, you know, he got it on the second pass. Two out of the three kids got hares that day. I'll never forget that. It was just one of those special days."

It's hard to miss the sentiment in Mary's voice as she goes on. "And that young kid is now an avid snowshoe hare hunter, who takes other kids out every year."

On the Allegheny, Mary found new habitats from what she was used to back home. "We don't have the cedar swamps here that we had back in Michigan," she says. "The snowshoes here are in the young successional forest, the regenerating timber harvests. That's where we find them."

Dr. Duane Diefenbach agrees. Diefenbach, a Penn State wildlife researcher, is conducting one of the first scientific studies ever of snowshoe hares in the Keystone State.

"It's one of those game species that we've been hunting for years," Diefenbach says, "but we don't know that much about it. We're trying to look at it on a very large scale, trying to see how common snowshoe hares are in the northern tier."

Echoing Hosmer, Diefenbach points out that, "we have so little conifer cover compared to other states. [Hare habitat in Pennsylvania] would have to be a thick regenerating hardwood stand, maybe with laurel nearby as a surrogate for conifer cover."

I thought of the snowshoe hare I had seen in bear season. It was crouched in a regenerating stand of hardwoods.

When asked if hunting affects snowshoe hare populations here, Diefenbach says, "I highly doubt hunting has any impact on the overall population. I can't imagine that the amount that's going on statewide has any effect at all. Not very many people hunt them here."

Try telling that to Mary and our hunting partners for the day, Nate Welker and Rob Musi. Welker, like Hosmer, is a USFS biologist and an avid beagler. An Army veteran, Welker used his GI money to get a Masters in Biology from Tennessee Tech when he returned stateside. After working as a biologist for the Pennsylvania Department of Environmental Protection, he moved to the Forest Service a few years ago.

Musi also has a degree in biology, but he puts his science background to work as a school teacher. As a young college graduate he was looking for work in his field when a teaching position opened up at a district near the Allegheny. "When I saw how close it was to the National Forest," Musi told me as we walked through the woods, "I figured I couldn't pass that up." He liked both the teaching and the surroundings so much that he's been here ever since.

On Mary's advice, the four of us were hunting a recent timber cut just a few miles west of Marienville. This was a new hunting spot for her, but during a tour of the site earlier in the fall she had seen a couple of snowshoe hares. With the hit-or-miss nature of hare populations in this region, that was as good a lead as any.

Due to about two inches of slushy snowfall and freezing rain the night before, the going was slow on the unpaved roads. As a result, our parade of trucks didn't reach the timber cut until nearly 11 AM. After we parked, Welker opened the back of his SUV and popped open a crate. Out sprang his two low-slung beagles, Lee and Mouse.

Like most beagles, Welker's boys didn't waste much time socializing. They set immediately to siphoning up great nosefuls of scent from the snowy ground. They were ready to hunt much sooner than we were.

Our first spot consisted of piles of cut trees and brush, with just a little new growth starting up. The snow was too sloppy to find tracks, but Hosmer showed me several spots where hares had nibbled the bark from the bases of young trees. "That's what they eat when there's no understory browse available, or in the winter when it's covered by snow," she explained.

Like Mary, I grew up hunting over beagles, only we worked them for cottontails in western Pennsylvania's farm country. I shared her nostalgia as I watched the two stubby dogs work their way feverishly under, over, and through the timber piles.

As hard as they labored, though, they never got the chance to break into the sweet baying song that signifies a hound on a hot trail. The only baying came from Welker who occasionally called, "Lee, Mouse, he-ya," in a bass tone so deep that it could have done double duty as a ship's horn.

We completed our unsuccessful loop through the timber cut and walked back toward the trucks. As we strolled along talking, the dogs suddenly veered off the trail to investigate the low-hanging branches of a small clump of pines. They didn't spend much time, only a few seconds, but Welker knew his boys well – it was enough to convince him to take a closer look.

He took about three steps toward the trees when a grouse burst from below the branches. We swung our shotguns in unison, but the bird managed to keep the dense pines directly in its wake as it winged away down the valley. None of us ever saw it.

Stymied, we decided to try a slightly older regenerating clearcut that we had passed on the drive in. This promising spot was much thicker and at one point, for about three minutes, the hair on my arms and neck stood at attention as the beagles gave tongue. We could hear them running a trail as they bayed, but Welker eventually decided that they were chasing a deer and called them off. Despite the excitement, the end result was the same: no hares.

As a last ditch effort, we tried a brush patch that fell somewhere between the first two in age. The cover was far more open, with only a few large trees left standing (called a "shelterwood" cut by foresters, most of the trees in a stand are cut, but a few mature ones are left to spread seeds and help regeneration). Most of the patch was dense blackberry canes, goldenrod, and crowded stands of maple and black birch saplings. It looked like excellent habitat, but we were shut out again.

By 2:30, we were ready to call it quits. As Welker and Mary pulled out, Musi asked if I wanted to finish out the day muzzleloader hunting. He told me he had a spot in mind that wasn't far away, and that we would be able to get in at least 90 minutes of hunting before dark.

I debated whether I wanted to stay, reminding myself that I still had guests at home. But Musi's offer was enticing and the thought of the celebration that would ensue if I pulled into the driveway with a deer in the bed of the pickup was too tempting. I caved in.

The spot he took me to was just north of Salmon Creek, west of Marienville. Musi explained that this used to be his regular deer hunting spot till about 10 years ago. "It used to be pretty good back then," he said hopefully.

As we walked together up the mountainside, Musi noted that the area had changed significantly due to the installation of gas wells. There were two new access roads and at least four new wells on the hillside that Musi wanted to hunt.

Mary Hosmer is fond of pointing out that the USFS staff on the Allegheny prefers to work with oil and gas drillers to get something back for the Forest when those companies access the resources that belong to them. "The National Forest is not managed to produce money," she says. "It's managed to produce outputs to serve the public. Recreation is a good example. Where do people want to go on the Forest? They use the [oil and gas well] roads to get there."

Our muzzleloader hunt proved her point. When Musi and I separated partway up the mountain, I stayed on the access road because, without knowing where I was or, for that matter, where I was headed, it was a convenient way to keep from getting lost.

In the hollows along Salmon Creek, the temperatures had stayed lower on this sunless day and the snow was more suitable for tracking. I cut several sets of tracks, but with limited daylight and no knowledge of the terrain, I was reluctant to chase them down. Instead, I still-hunted along the road, occasionally veering into the thick brush and grapevine tangles bordering it.

With about a half-hour of daylight left, I hadn't seen any deer, nor had I run into Musi again. I was now on the back side of the ridge, so I decided to cut across the crest and drop back down to the road below. As I walked past a gas well, I encountered the blue blazes designating this segment of the access road as part of the North Country Trail. On a whim, I chose to follow it.

I had walked about 100 yards along the trail when suddenly, from the thick black birch saplings below me, two deer leapt to their feet. The stock of the Pennsylvania rifle snapped to my shoulder in a familiar motion as I tracked the running deer to my left.

I was fairly sure the lead deer was a buck although I hadn't gotten a clear look at its head. The second one, though, was unmistakably a doe.

After their first hasty jumps, the pair now slowed to a hurried walk. I could pick out the doe through the leafy saplings every few steps, but I couldn't get a clean shot.

Both time and distance were now working against me. I knew from the gathering gloom that I was up against the end of legal shooting hours. On top of that, the deer were angling away from me and each step made any potential shot longer.

Needing to take a chance, I bleated at the pair. The doe jerked to a halt and stared.

It was, as they say, the moment of truth. She was 70 yards away and downhill. On top of that she had managed to stop with some brush squarely between her and me.

The creeping darkness sided with the deer. I found myself squinting down the barrel of the long rifle trying to distinguish between leaves and deer hide. Much as I strained to, I couldn't.

A rush of thoughts went through my mind. I could see her head, so I could guess at her shoulder location and take a shot through the brush. But if she ran off after a bad shot, it would mean tracking her through the dark woods in unfamiliar territory; I had been down that road once already this fall. I could also try a head shot, but that was almost a sure miss here in the gloaming.

Seconds ticked by. The doe's ears twitched. She was ready to bolt.

I pulled the rifle down.

It was a wrenching decision. I desperately wanted to take a deer with my muzzleloader here on the Allegheny. But, as I walked down the mountain in the dark, I realized my choice was the right one.

When I got back to the trucks, Musi was there waiting for me. He told me that he had seen lots of sign, but no deer, and I quickly recapped what had happened at last light. With that we parted ways and drove toward home.

The day had packed quite a bit of activity into just nine hours of daylight and my eyes were now drooping. On top of that, I was still a little annoyed at having to pass up the shot.

But when I thought of the diminutive Lee and Mouse bawling up the trail, a small grin came to my face. And when I reached back once again to yesterday's waterfowl hunt with Dan my smile widened even more.

I realized that I had a lot to be thankful for this holiday season, both at home and here in the Forest. And, with my family gathered close and with more hunting days on the

Allegheny yet to come, I knew that there was much more still ahead.

CHAPTER 12

REGENERATION

Like Mary Hosmer on her best-ever snowshoe hare hunt and John Mack at his Youth Pheasant Hunt, one of the greatest thrills I get from hunting is watching the smiles of youngsters as they discover for the first time the joys of life in the field. Over the years I've had the opportunity to help several young people as they've bagged their first pheasant or dropped their first deer, and it fills me with a particular kind of joy and pride that I haven't found anywhere else.

Although my own kids have not yet reached Pennsylvania's legal hunting age, all three of them have accompanied me on hunts. I try to make sure that the experience doesn't become too grueling for them, and that it's interesting and educational too.

I hoped to let them share my adventures on the Allegheny, but this was a bit problematic. I knew that Stephanie (9 years old) and Jake (5) were too young to tolerate the early wake-up call and the three-hour drive that an Allegheny National Forest hunt demanded, let alone the long walks and potential for bad weather. They were going to have to sit this one out.

Eleven-year old Rachel, though, was a different story. Fascinated with hunting virtually all her life, and now just a year short of getting her license, she had been lobbying hard to join me. Plus, she is a burgeoning distance runner with the stamina to hunt all day, and she has her father's ignorance of the inconveniences of being cold and wet (said another way, she doesn't know when to come in out of the rain either).

In short, Rachel was in.

We left two hours before dawn on January 8, intent on chasing pheasants at Buzzard Swamp. Dan Fitzgerald, having recuperated from our Clarion River duck hunt, planned to meet us there, but when my cell phone rang at 6:15 AM, I knew he wasn't going to make it. As a railroad engineer, his travel schedule is determined by the trains and he was hung up miles from home. When I snapped shut the phone, I told Rachel, "Well, it's just you and me."

On the ride north, she curled into a tiny ball and slept. Hunter dozed half in the back seat and half in the front, with his muzzle perched in an uncomfortable-looking position on the console between Rachel and me.

The temperature was hovering around 32 degrees and, with the gloomy skies overhead, I kept hoping that it would drop.

Unfortunately, it was not to be and as we rolled into Marienville, a gray rain soaked the Christmas decorations that still clung to light poles and porch railings.

When scouting Buzzard Swamp for my early season goose hunt, I talked to PGC Wildlife Conservation Officer Mario Piccirilli, who surprised me when he said, "It's one of our best spots up here for pheasant hunting."

Pheasants? "There are some really big areas where we've planted warm season grasses out there and we're starting to see some evidence that some of the birds we're stocking there are overwintering."

I asked how Buzzard Swamp compared to the Beanfield when it came to ringnecks on the Allegheny. "Oh, we stock way more pheasants down there than they do at the Beanfield," he replied. "Plus, I think our reproducing population is bigger too."

USFS biologist Pam Thurston explained to me that warm season grass fields have been planted between the water impoundments at Buzzard Swamp, allowing a reproducing population of pheasants to establish there. And, as frequently seems to be the case on the Allegheny, it's hunters that have done the heavy lifting.

"[The warm season grass plantings] are a result of the cooperative efforts of the PGC and the National Wild Turkey Federation, among others [including Ducks Unlimited]," she said.

Their efforts are starting to pay off, Thurston told me, and biologists are starting to see some overwintering birds. "That has only been the case over the last five years," she noted, pointing out that this exactly coincides with the warm season grass planting program.

Two years ago, after one of the most severe winters in recent memory, Thurston figured the fledgling Buzzard Swamp pheasant population was doomed. But, come springtime, the birds were alive and well, nestled safely among the switchgrass and big bluestem plantings. "Everything points to the fact that [the pheasant population at Buzzard Swamp] is there for good," she concluded.

Remembering that I had flushed two pheasants here during my earlier visit, I hoped Buzzard Swamp might create a perfect hunting day for Rachel, Hunter, and me. Instead, it was a miserable mess.

Blue-gray clouds alternately dispensed rain and sleet, forming a one-inch crust of ice on top of the slushy snow. The ice wasn't strong enough to support us and worse, it yanked at our boots, making each step feel like we were battling the jaws of a steel trap.

The going was even tougher for Hunter. Bothered by a reoccurrence of the pad problem that had plagued him back in November, he was soon slowed to a walk by the broken, jagged ice. Then spots of blood began to appear in his paw prints.

Within an hour we were drenched to the skin. We had seen only one ringneck and couldn't even get a shot at him when he flushed well out of range.

When reached the far end of Buzzard Swamp's trails, I had had enough of fighting the mess from the sky and on the ground. I was soaked and annoyed, Hunter was limping, and even Rachel, game as she had been all morning, was ready to get give in.

On the way out, I showed Rachel the spot where Hunter and I crouched in the tall grass waiting for geese and pointed out numerous sets of deer tracks in the snow. We also found a set of day-old grouse tracks along the trail and, as we veered off the path to let Hunter nose around them a bit, we stumbled across snowshoe hare tracks too. Both sets were crusted and caved in from the morning's weather, so we didn't bother following them any further.

Just before we reached the parking lot, a gray squirrel darted across the path. Rachel begged me to shoot him so we would have at least something to show for our miserable morning. Unfortunately the gray had gone from left to right in front of us, which took him into the protection of the wildlife propagation area. It was literally the luckiest day of that squirrel's life because it could have easily been his last.

I took the opportunity to explain to my daughter that the propagation area offered him a sanctuary and why that sanctuary is so important to the wildlife that lives in Buzzard Swamp and beyond. Although I want my children to grow up to enjoy hunting, it is critical to me that they understand that the hunter's first responsibility is not to himself or his pursuit, but to the game animals themselves and the conservation of their habitat.

It's this ethic, after all, that shaped the habitat at Buzzard Swamp and enabled it to house the many species we had encountered: pheasants, grouse, snowshoe hare, deer, geese, ducks, turkeys, and bear, all in one place. This code of conservation characterizes not only the hunter-based groups that are so active across the Allegheny, but also pioneers like Theodore Roosevelt, who embraced the vision and then created the reality of the National Forest system that we experience today.

In an excellent essay about Roosevelt's conservation ethic, Ken Barrett of the Theodore Roosevelt Conservation Partnership (a hunter and angler-based conservation group that adopted Roosevelt's name to indicate their particular interest in public lands) writes, "During his presidency TR set aside 230 million acres of public lands, establishing in the process numerous National Forests, National Parks, National Wildlife Refuges and Monuments. One historian observed that it amounted to one acre of land for every second he was president! Today, the majority of the 230 million acres is open to the public for hunting and fishing, and serves as the bulwark for the greatest public lands estate in the world."[48]

Long before his presidency, Roosevelt was a passionate hunter. In 1887, he teamed with *Forest and Stream* (precursor of *Field and Stream*) editor George Bird Grinnell to found the Boone and Crockett Club, which would serve as both an outdoorsmen's society and a conservation tool. Grinnell's editorial pages had been sounding the clarion call for forest management and natural resource conservation for years, and the Boone and Crockett Club supported these concepts as part of the hunting lifestyle.

When Roosevelt was elected president in 1904, he carried his conservation ethic to the nation. One of his first acts in office was the creation of the US Forest Service to oversee "forest reserves" (the name was changed to "National Forests" in 1907). Though a few forest reserves had been in place since1891, the Forest Service would now have more direction and discretion over their use.

Roosevelt named Gifford Pinchot his first Chief of the US Forest Service. Pinchot shared TR's passion for hunting and the outdoors, and was the first person to study forestry at an American university. When he enrolled at Yale in 1885, "I had no more conception of what it meant to be a forester than the man in the moon. But at least a forester worked in the woods and with the woods – and I loved the woods and everything about them."[49]

Pinchot – who later became governor of Pennsylvania, taking office in 1923, the same year in which the Allegheny was designated – had already bought into the code of conservation and was preaching it at every turn. As he later wrote, "When the Gay Nineties began, the common word for our forests was 'inexhaustible'...The few friends the forest had were spoken of, when they were spoken of at all, as impractical theorists, fanatics, or 'denuditics,' more or less touched in the head. What talk there was about forest protection was no more to the average American than the buzzing of a mosquito, and just about as irritating."[50]

These attitudes, along with a dearth of governmental protection, decimated forest resources nationwide. Predictably, the timber blitz had a corresponding effect on wildlife populations and by 1900 there were less than a half-million white-tailed deer nationwide; fewer than 100,000 wild turkeys; and just 41,000 elk.[51]

With the power of the federal government behind them, Roosevelt and Pinchot set about changing those numbers and the attitudes that begat them. When the Forest Service was created in 1905 there were 60 forest reserves. With Pinchot practically guiding his hand, Roosevelt's pen strokes consigned tract after tract to federal ownership, creating 150 new National Forests over the next four years.

Roosevelt and Pinchot saw the National Forest system not for preservation – TR was busy adding National Game Preserves, National Parks, National Monuments, and Federal Bird Reserves for that purpose – but for conservation, using the Forests slowly and carefully so that their presence would be continuously assured. To the Forest Service's credo of "Greatest Good for the Greatest Number," Pinchot added the phrase "In the Long Run," to underline his belief in the conservation ethic.[52]

These two pioneering conservationists changed the face of the nation by adding 120 million acres of National Forest to our landscape. But more than that, they changed our consciousness.

They inspired legislation such as the 1911 Weeks Act, which authorized the purchase of National Forests not only in the largely undeveloped West, but also in the East- like the Allegheny. They motivated hunter-conservationists like Aldo Leopold to stretch the Forest Service's role even further in the interest of wildlife and game management. And they placed in the souls of all outdoorsmen the concept that they could be individually responsible for stewardship of forest resources.

Doug Painter, president of the National Shooting Sports Foundation, said of TR and his new breed of hunter-conservationists, "Without Roosevelt and hunters to carry on his outdoor spirit, the American culture might have very different values today. Most of us know the thrill of seeing and hearing ducks, geese, wild turkey, deer and elk. Unfortunately, far fewer people understand that these species were saved from extinction, and thrive today, because of conservation...by hunters."

Naturally, things haven't always been rosy between hunters and the Forest Service. In the 1960s, for example, turkey hunters pushed a federal lawsuit that led to the National Forest Management Act of 1976, requiring the USFS to take into consideration a diversity of plant and animal species in their planning processes.[53]

But today, the level of cooperation between hunters and the USFS may be at an all time high: the USFS's Dennis Daniel operates out of National Wild Turkey Federation's national office; the Ruffed Grouse Society leaps to the defense of the USFS in lawsuits; and these and other groups - Ducks

Unlimited, Pheasants Forever, and the Rocky Mountain Elk Foundation, to name a few – contribute millions of dollars annually to improve wildlife habitat on National Forests and Grasslands.

It is exactly this kind of understanding of the need for continuous habitat improvement, this ongoing commitment to conservation, that I want to instill in my children. I want them to remember that the National Forests are ours and that, to honor the legacy of pioneers like Roosevelt, Grinnell, Pinchot, and Leopold – and, perhaps more so, to honor our obligation to the animals we choose to hunt – we must be conservative in what we take from the Forests and liberal in what we put back.

I was preaching some passage from this gospel to Rachel when we arrived back in Marienville, but it was hard to tell how much of it was getting past the sound of her chattering teeth. Her long, dark hair hung in dripping clumps from under the drenched safety orange ballcap she had gotten for Christmas. Needing a place to get her warm and dry, I bypassed my usual gas station food for a sit-down meal at the Bucktail Hotel.

We walked through the door as strangers, but owner Barbara Kuhl greeted us like neighbors, asking brightly, "How are you today?"

"Wet," I replied grumpily. "Wet and hungry."

"Well go sit over there then," she said cheerfully, pointing to a table at the side window, "by the heat register. Take your boots and socks off if you want to warm up."

Rachel looked uncertainly at me as we sat down. She knew full well that under normal circumstances I would no more let her take her boots and socks off in a public eatery than I would decide to dine bare-chested myself. I picked up her uneasy glance and considered the situation for a moment.

I knew her feet had to be freezing. I looked around the restaurant, empty except for us and the staff. "Go ahead," I said, "Take your boots off and set them by the heater to dry."

"Are you sure?" she asked, still a bit shy about this bit of permissible impropriety.

"Are your feet cold?" I asked.

"Yeah, they're freezing 'cause my socks and my boots are soaked," she answered quickly.

"Then get them off," I said. I knew she had clean socks in the truck, but I figured the drier we could get her boots, the more comfortable the ride home would be for her.

Once we were situated I ordered the ½-pound Bucktail Burger and a bowl of chili, and Rachel went to work on an order of chicken fingers. As we devoured our meal, I noticed her looking around the room at the antique pictures and knick-knacks on the shelves.

"What are you thinking about?" I asked after a bit.

"I was just thinking that if we ever get a restaurant, I want it to be just like this," she said.

"Are we planning to buy a restaurant?" I asked in mock surprise. "Is there something you and Mom were planning that I didn't hear about?"

"Dad!" she answered with laughing exasperation. "No-o-o. I just mean if we ever *did* decide to buy a restaurant, this is how I would like it to be. You know, with lots of old stuff on the walls and really nice people working there."

"I'll make a note of it," I said, "For when we do decide to go restaurant shopping."

As we worked our way through the huge servings, Barbara came over to chat. She asked what we were hunting for and whether we had had any luck, then talked about the fact that hunters only seem to stop in during bear and deer season.

"A lot of them," she said, "hunt out of camps, you know. I think they just bring everything they need along with them from home and they don't go out much." At this time of year, she informed us, the Bucktail's business is much more dependent upon snowmobilers and ATV riders.

While I polished off Rachel's leftover French fries, Barbara gave her a quick tour of the restaurant. When the pair came back to the table, Barbara asked her, "Well, what do you think?"

"I like it," Rachel enthused, "I really like it a lot!" Then she added, with a look over at me, "But this is the first time I ever ate with my shoes off in a restaurant!" Our laughter rippled across the empty room.

Soon, I looked at my watch and realized that we had spent over two hours at the Bucktail.

"Are you ready to go home?" I asked Rachel.

"Aw-w-w-w," she whined, switching instantly to preteen moaning mode. "Do we have to?"

"Ye-e-e-e-s," I crooned back. "If we don't leave soon, I think they're going to toss us out anyway."

"No, I meant, do we have to go home? I wanted to go hunting some more."

"Oh." I was taken aback. I had simply assumed that, tired, cold, and wet – and now with a full belly – she would be ready for a long nap on the ride home.

"Well, I don't know," I said slowly. "Why don't you go in and go to the bathroom before we leave?"

"I don't really have to go."

"Just go. It'll be a long time before we have another chance."

This classic parental stalling tactic gave me time to ponder my options. I certainly didn't mind going out again, but I didn't want to make it a chore for Rachel. On the other hand, the morning's lousy weather and abysmal results certainly hadn't crushed her spirits.

"OK," I said when she returned from the restroom looking expectantly at me, "We'll try hunting again as long as

Hunter's feet aren't bothering him too much. If they are, we'll pack up and go."

"Cool!" was her only reply.

I went out to the F-150 to grab some dry socks for Rachel and to snag my Allegheny National Forest Hunting Map. I wasn't up for the long walk required by another Buzzard Swamp engagement, so I needed to find someplace else, preferably someplace close. Luckily, the Hunting Map designates recent timber cuts, which makes it an excellent guide for grouse hunters. I found a spot a few miles north of Marienville, just off of Route 66.

When we pulled into the snowy parking area, I told Rachel that this was going to be a little tougher than the pheasant hunting that she was used to. She assured me she was up to the challenge.

I laid out a course on the map that would loop us to the north and then east, bringing us back to the truck. A check of Hunter's pads told me that they weren't bad, but I still didn't want to be at this too long.

The hunt itself was uneventful. Although the cover was decent, there seemed to be little grouse food and we had no flushes. The sole excitement came when I missed our return point to the truck by a couple hundred yards. It added only about 20 minutes to our trip, but to Rachel's young imagination we were wandering lost in the wilds and only miraculously found our way back. The adventure was heightened when a large doe bolted across the road just a few yards in front of us.

As we covered the last few paces toward the F-150, another truck rolled slowly down the isolated road. We waved and, in the timeless tradition of end-of-the-day hunters, they stopped to chat.

"Did you do any good?" asked the driver.

"It was a long day," I replied, "but nothing to show for it."

"Same here," he agreed, adding that they had been muzzleloader hunting for deer. "Did you have fun?" he asked, looking past me to Rachel.

"Yeah!" she said excitedly. "We didn't see any grouse, but a deer just ran across the road in front of us! And this morning we saw some grouse tracks and snowshoe hare tracks. And a pheasant, but he was too far away and we couldn't get him."

Listening to her breathless recap, it dawned on me that many of the things that I take for granted in the outdoors were new and fresh to her.

"She's cute," said the driver to me, half under his breath. "And that's a beautiful dog."

"Thanks," I said appreciatively.

His partner looked across from the passenger side of the truck. "Looks like you've got two good hunting partners there," he said with a wide smile.

"Yeah," I said, realizing what a truly excellent day this had actually been.

I tossed my arm around Rachel's shoulders and pulled her snugly to my side. "Yeah, I do."

CHAPTER 13

HOWLING WILDERNESS

In contrast to social affairs like waterfowl, snowshoe hare, and upland bird hunting, my next hunt on the Allegheny would be a private matter: just my flintlock and me. Still smarting from my muzzleloader disappointment on the Tionesta tract, I went in search of a new venue, one that would match the backwoods expectations that I had in mind.

My first thought was the 8,663-acre Hickory Creek Wilderness. I placed a quick call to Mary Hosmer to get her opinion of the idea.

"Oh, you don't want to hunt deer there," she said emphatically. "There aren't many deer there at all compared to other areas on the Forest. In fact, the Hickory Creek Wilderness isn't really very good for any kind of hunting." Then Mary added a truly thought-provoking statement.

"Keep in mind," she said, "that Wilderness Areas are managed for the people, not for the animals."

Some experts claim that Wilderness preserves are an absolute necessity for scientific study, backcountry recreation, and biodiversity preservation. Others, like Mary, argue that Wilderness designations are a concept fabricated for romantic rather than realistic motives.

Of course, the subject of wilderness and its place in our world has elicited varying opinions for centuries. For example, in the 1760s, as the first settlers crept west of the Allegheny Mountains, the frontiersman found "an unknown region, and surrounded with dangers...He did not know at what tread his foot might be stung by a serpent, at what moment he might meet with the formidable bear, or if in the evening, he knew not on what limb of a tree, over his head, the murderous panther might be perched, in a squatting attitude, to drop down upon him and tear him to pieces in a moment."[54]

One hundred years later, though, the perception of wilderness in some circles had reversed itself. The Transcendentalists, led by Ralph Waldo Emerson and Henry David Thoreau, postulated that we should embrace nature and that its return embrace would have a restorative effect on our souls. "We can love nothing but nature," Emerson wrote, "nearness or likeness of nature, — how beautiful is the ease of its victory!"[55]

For his part, Thoreau opined that, "Generally speaking, a howling wilderness does not howl: it is the imagination of the traveler that does the howling."[56] He then called for "a primitive forest, of five hundred or a thousand acres, either in one body or several – where a stick should never be cut for fuel – nor for the navy, nor to make wagons, but stand and decay for higher uses – a common possession forever..."[57]

In the 150 years since Emerson and Thoreau, the concept of wilderness has evolved as something to be valued, and further, protected – both for the enjoyment of humans and the intrinsic value of the wilderness itself. This ideal was noted in the language of the Wilderness Act: "A wilderness, in contrast with those areas where man and his works dominate the landscape, is hereby recognized as an area where the earth and its community of life are untrammeled by man, where man himself is a visitor who does not remain."

One modern voice that contradicts this post-Transcendental Wilderness point of view is that of J. Baird Callicott, a professor of philosophy and religion studies at the University of North Texas. Callicott suggests that "Wilderness is, in short, a 'socially constructed' idea," founded in the fact that "[b]y the middle of the nineteenth century, undespoiled nature was becoming so scarce in the heartland of Puritan America, that Thoreau felt compelled to call for its deliberate preservation."[58]

In Callicott's opinion, "'Wilderness' is not a name like 'mountain' or 'river' that refers to common features of nature, but a lens through which nature is perceived."

From that perspective, he advocates for sustainable, ecologically sensitive development rather than the romanticized notion of preserving, or even creating, wilderness.

I would suggest that wilderness is not a lens to view nature, but society – and its proximity to wild lands and wildlife – is the lens through which wilderness is perceived. Historically, it seems that those immersed in wilderness, the people dealing with the very real struggles and dangers of life in the backcountry, viewed it like the settlers on the Pennsylvania frontier, as an obstacle and a source of fear.

But as observers became more removed from real wilderness, the kind that housed crouching panthers and armed Indians, the absence created a fondness in their hearts. Thoreau's opinion on "howling wilderness," for instance, was penned only about 15 years after three dozen people from a single wagon train froze or starved to death while crossing the Sierra Nevada Mountains. It seems doubtful that the surviving members of the Donner Party would agree with his assessment that howling wilderness was a figment of their imagination.

People facing the very real possibility of injury or death from the wilderness or its inhabitants lack control over their situation; as a result, the wilderness becomes an object of terror and they heighten their attempts control it. Those geographically – or in more modern times, technologically – removed from the reality of wilderness danger find it painless to wax poetic at its beauty and strength.

This applies equally to the nineteenth century Transcendentalists of the industrial, urban East or the inhabitants of the industrial, urban United States of today.

Our lives are safe and controlled in ways that drive us not just to idealize wilderness, but to seek it out to invigorate our otherwise stale existence. In that way, wilderness becomes just another X-Games venue, whether the thrill you're seeking comes from rock climbing on Weaver's Needle in Arizona's Superstition Wilderness or floating the Boundary Waters Canoe Area Wilderness in Minnesota.

Despite my background as a scientist, I have sometimes constructed my own romantic image of nature and its wild qualities too. I have frequently spent time seeking out the backcountry, especially when I'm hunting white-tailed deer with my flintlock rifle. At those times, I'm seeking to make a connection to another era, reaching through a woodland portal to a distant time when my ancestors first traveled this 'unknown region.'

Perhaps critics like Callicott would suggest that in these instances the wilderness is less of a setting than a set, a backdrop upon which my vision of hunting the undespoiled nature of my forebears can be played out. I'll concede that that may be true. However, it's an unscripted vision, one over which I have little control, and therefore still an authentic experience.

Authentic or not, I still wanted an opportunity to see deer while I was hunting. Based on Mary's counsel, I scrapped Hickory Creek and decided to find a touch of wilderness the old-fashioned way: I pulled out a map and looked for the place that had the least roads.

The spot that caught my eye was in the upper right corner of the National Forest, tucked against the New York state line.

Designated as part of the Allegheny National Recreation Area, this roadless area wraps around the 12,500-acre Allegheny Reservoir. The eastern part of this untrammeled area is called Tracy Ridge.

Tracy Ridge is the centerpiece of a roughly 9,000-acre roadless area, one of the largest remaining on the Allegheny. Nearly 20 miles from the nearest town, this area is so remote that an astronomical society called Dark Sky Observing identified it as one of the best areas in Pennsylvania to stargaze away from city lights.

But astronomers are not the only group interested in Tracy Ridge. When the 1986 Forest Plan was put into place, this was one of the sites evaluated for Wilderness designation and when it didn't make the cut, it was instead designated as part of the Allegheny National Recreation Area.

As they update their Forest Plan, the Forest Service is addressing Wilderness designations once again and in an effort to shove that issue to the forefront, a group called Friends of Allegheny Wilderness (FAW) has put together a proposal to designate an additional 54,460 acres on the Allegheny. Among these areas are the virgin forest of the Tionesta tract, the roadless area along the north shore of the Wild and Scenic Clarion River, and Tracy Ridge.

Ironically, one of FAW's primary arguments for adding Wilderness focuses not on biodiversity or aesthetics, but statistics. "The Hickory Creek and Allegheny Islands Wilderness Areas combined make up less than two percent of the land area of the Allegheny," says FAW Executive Director Kirk Johnson. By comparison, the percentage of

Wilderness across the entire National Forest System is 18 percent and in the Eastern Region the number is about 11 percent.

"That's not a justification for adding more Wilderness," Johnson told me, "but it's more to illustrate that there is room for improvement on the Allegheny. That's such a significant disparity that I think it's relevant to look at that statistic."

FAW says that they are not trying to stop resource use on the Allegheny. Their report states: "We recognize that timber management and oil and gas development are important and appropriate uses of the ANF, and we support the continuation of these practices...We believe it is possible to move a significant amount of ANF acreage into [Wilderness designation]...without significantly affecting the levels of timber harvesting in the Forest, and without trauma to the timber or oil and gas industries..."

To this proclamation, Johnson adds that "it's clear to people that we've gone out of our way in selecting sites that avoid conflicts with other multiple uses. I would say most people in extractive industries see that there's room for compromise." He adds that the loud anti-logging positions of groups like the Sierra Club and the Allegheny Defense Project have been "the biggest impediment to getting Wilderness designation because it's created an atmosphere of distrust."

FAW's proposal also sees hunting as a key component within Wilderness Areas, stating unequivocally that "FAW supports hunting and fishing in Wilderness," and adding a now-familiar refrain on the value of hunters on the Forest: "The hunting community will likely play an important role in moving the forest cover in new ANF wilderness toward late-successional and old-growth conditions by helping to control the deer population."

In Johnson's view, this is another thing that sets FAW apart from the Allegheny Defense Project. "There's more of an animal rights crowd you can find associated with ADP, which is a pretty significant difference from us," he says. "Part of the reason why we're proposing this is to provide a wilderness hunting experience."

On a mid-January morning, I set out for Tracy Ridge in search of just such an experience although I carried a healthy dose of uncertainty. For one thing, the temperature the day before had been an unbelievably toasty 72 degrees – not exactly what I was hoping for on a late season deer hunt. Overnight, however, the mercury had plunged. Given the odd winter winds that sometimes swirl around the Allegheny Reservoir, I wondered what conditions would be awaiting my arrival.

Another question was my health. I woke that morning with a searing backache, probably a belated gift from my 39th birthday the week before. My throbbing upper back and neck seemed to drag me ever slower as I clomped around the house that morning preparing for the trip. I got started nearly an hour late and, as I stretched, twisted, and heaved my shoulders in a futile attempt to stay comfortable behind the wheel, I wondered how long I would be able to tote my heavy Pennsylvania long rifle through the woods.

Three hours into the drive, I passed Camp Stockert then crossed Kinzua Creek at the southern tip of the Allegheny Reservoir. Nearly an hour later, I reached Sugar Bay, another arm of the reservoir. Consulting my map, I realized that I had not even covered half of the 24-mile length of the giant water body. Obviously, with 12,000 acres of surface water and 91 miles of shoreline, I knew it was large, but I didn't really comprehend how big until I tried to drive around it.

The Allegheny Reservoir is held back by the 179-foot high Kinzua Dam, which was once the largest structure of its kind in the northeastern US. Located about eight miles upriver from the city of Warren and about 200 miles above Pittsburgh, the dam was dedicated on September 17, 1966, nearly four decades after it was first proposed.[59] The reasons for that delay still tarnish the record of United States public works projects – and government relations with American Indians.

To construct the $120 million project, the US Army Corps of Engineers had to purchase a total of 36 miles of railroad, 60 miles of roadway, eight miles of power lines, and six entire towns. None of these parcels, however, caused anything close to the nationwide outcry spurred by the acquisition of property belonging to the Seneca Indian Nation, descendants of the tribe that once occupied Buckaloons and formed the western end of the Iroquois longhouse.

In the late 1700s, when the Iroquois were still a powerful military force, the war chief of the Seneca was a man named Gy-ant-wa-hia, or Cornplanter. Although he had been commissioned as a captain in the British army during the American Revolution, Cornplanter elected to seek an amicable settlement with the Americans at the close of the war. In appreciation of his diligent efforts to seek peace between the Seneca and frontier settlers, the state of Pennsylvania granted Cornplanter and his heirs several parcels of land, including a 1000-acre tract along the west bank of the Allegheny River.

Shortly thereafter, President George Washington commissioned treaty talks to end conflicts between the Iroquois Confederacy and the American settlers who were now swarming west over the Allegheny Mountains. The resultant Pickering Treaty of 1794 established a 30,000-acre Seneca Reservation in New York, starting at the Pennsylvania/New York state line and extending north along both sides of the Allegheny River.

The treaty promised "free use and enjoyment" of the land as the "property of the Seneca Nation; and [that] the United States will never claim [ownership]." This treaty allowed the tribe to have a permanent home, while their rights to Pennsylvania's Cornplanter Grant let them maintain possession of one of their most sacred shrines, the site on which Cornplanter's half-brother, Handsome Lake, founded the modern Seneca religion.

For over a century Cornplanter and his descendants lived quietly along the banks of the upper Allegheny – until a series of floods along the Allegheny River between 1905 and 1928 brought the in US Army Corps of Engineers. Attempting to stem the inundation and protect villages and cities downstream, the Corps developed three different flood control proposals: a canal and a series of smaller dams along major Allegheny River tributaries, a canal that would divert the river to Lake Erie, or a high dam on the upper part of the river.

Battle lines were quickly and distinctly drawn. Those who lived along the upper Allegheny, including the Seneca Nation and residents of Warren, favored diverting the river; the Pittsburgh contingent opposed diversion and favored the high dam. For nearly 30 years squabbling continued and no solution was near, until 1956, when nature intervened.

In that year, flood tides came once again to the Allegheny, but this time they swept as far upstream as the city of Warren. After sharing the shocking destructive force of the river's deluge, the upriver communities instantly swung their allegiances and cried out for a dam to be built immediately. At last everyone was united behind the cause of constructing a dam on the upper Allegheny. Everyone, that is, except the Seneca.

With public and political forces aligned against them, the Indian nation battled tirelessly in every venue available to them. They took the fight into the courtrooms, all the way to the US Supreme Court; onto Capitol Hill, where they negotiated directly with Congress; and onto the pages and airwaves of the nation.

The Seneca opposed the dam not only because they would lose 10,000 acres of property, but also on religious and ethical grounds. The project would affect the holy Handsome Lake shrine; require the relocation of ancestral burial grounds, which the Seneca believed would destroy their ability to communicate with the gods through their dead relatives; and perhaps most significantly, it would inundate Cornplanter's gravesite.

It was the latter point that nationwide commentators seized upon and – with savvy assistance from groups like the American Civil Liberties Union – TV, radio, and print media were soon jammed with news releases and opinion pieces about the proposed Kinzua Dam.

The *New York Times* and *Washington Post* came out with editorials against the dam and in favor of the Seneca, as did the "Today" show.[60] Public figures, such as Congressmen John Phillips Saylor of Pennsylvania and James D. Haley of Florida, were named honorary members of the Seneca nation and radio debates were held with the Army Corps.

The most famous and lasting voice of support for the Seneca, however, came not from a politician, but from The Man in Black – country singer Johnny Cash. In 1964, Cash released the single *As Long As the Grass Shall Grow*, which dealt with the plight of the Seneca Reservation and Cornplanter's grave. The aching ballad paints a picture of deceit and shame:

After the US Revolution Cornplanter was a chief,

He told the tribe these men they could trust, that was his true belief,

He went down to Independence Hall and there was a treaty signed,

That promised peace with the USA and Indian rights combined...

On the Seneca Reservation there is much sadness now,

Washington's treaty has been broken and there is no hope no how,

Across the Allegheny River they're throwing up a dam,

It will flood the Indian country, a proud day for Uncle Sam...

The nationwide outcry was effective at bringing public attention to the Kinzua controversy, but sadly for the Seneca tribe, it had no effect on the ultimate outcome of the project. Beginning with a decision in the US District Court of Western New York in 1957, the Seneca lost round after round in court. Relentless and desperate, the tribe pushed their fight to the US Supreme Court, but on June 15, 1959 their motion to halt the federal acquisition of land was denied.

Despite support from Saylor and Haley, the Congressional fight went no better. When it was determined that the preferred alternative of the Seneca, diverting the river to Lake Erie, would increase project costs by at least 25 percent and require up to twice as much property acquisition, Congress quickly voted to appropriate funding for the Kinzua Dam, effectively ending the tribe's efforts on Capitol Hill.

Sensing that their options were nearly exhausted, the Seneca tried to make their cause a focal point of the 1960 Presidential campaign. But despite polite talk during the campaign, they soon found that the newly-elected Kennedy administration had no intention of stopping the project.

In August 1961 Kennedy told the Seneca Nation that he was sympathetic to their situation, but that the need for flood control on the Allegheny River would take priority.[61] It was the last blow in the fight over the Kinzua Dam.

Although there has been subsequent flood damage – most notably from Hurricane Agnes in 1972 and Hurricane Ivan in 2004 – there is no question that the Kinzua Dam has been effective in reducing impacts along the Allegheny Valley. Richard Dowling, a spokesman for the US Army Corps Pittsburgh District estimates that the dam has prevented nearly $1 billion in flood damage and saved "countless lives" since its construction.[62] However, the bitter battle over its construction has left lingering resentment on the part of the Seneca Nation.

George Heron, who was Seneca Nation president during the Kinzua controversy, said in a 2003 interview that the Kinzua clash taught them not to trust a government that ignored the oldest active Indian treaty.

"We fought it in the courts; we fought it in Congress," said Heron. "We fought it the best way we knew. We got a lot more out of it than if we hadn't fought it."[63]

And yet the dam stands today, a towering visual testament to a government effort as overwhelming and inevitable as the very floodwaters it was designed to hold back.

On my January drive to Tracy Ridge, the floodwaters from some of the smaller streams along the reservoir were barely under control. Icy patches and even flowing water showed up randomly on the road surface, making the drive rather more adventurous than I wanted. I eventually made it to Tracy Ridge, later than I had hoped, but excited nonetheless.

When I got out of the truck, the sun was shining brightly, but the temperature paid no attention to it. I guessed it to be in the high teens or low twenties.

I carefully poured a 75-grain load from the powder horn into my brass measure and emptied it down the neck of the sleek, black rifle barrel. Then I fished a patch out of the brass patch box in the rifle's stock, wrapped it around a lead ball, and tucked them both into the barrel's mouth. A couple of quick taps from my ball starter pushed the projectile a few inches down the barrel, and a few firm strokes from the ramrod set it firmly in place atop the powder charge.

I pulled my green wool pants over my jeans and tugged the familiar warmth of my Woolrich coat over my shoulders. For a bit of added warmth, I snugged a fleece gaiter around my neck. Although Pennsylvania does not require blaze orange during the late flintlock season – a nod to those who wish to recreate the past by dressing in buckskins or other colonial garb – I value my safety over historical accuracy, so I pulled on my blaze orange vest and hat.

As I walked up the entrance drive, I saw what I had hoped for most: a coat of snow had fallen overnight, four inches of fresh powder without a single blemish. The conditions would be perfect for tracking.

My plan for the day was almost no plan at all. I was simply going to roam the trails of Tracy Ridge and hope to see a deer or cut a set of deer tracks. If it was the latter, I intended to follow them until something dropped: the deer, the sun, or me.

Besides being a roadless area and a potential Wilderness, Tracy Ridge attracted me for other reasons. First, two of the streams that I would be following had names that immediately jumped out at me. For someone who was looking to reach back in time, the names Johnnycake Run and Whisky Run could have hardly been more appropriate.

Johnnycake is a baked flat cake of cornmeal mixed with milk, water, and eggs. For hungry eighteenth century pioneers, it was a sort of frontier energy bar. Whisky, of course, was the drink of choice of frontiersmen, especially the Scotch-Irish who were among the first to come over the Allegheny Mountains. The spirit served as libation, medicine, and currency among other things. It was so prized west of the mountains that the introduction of an excise tax in 1794 touched off an insurrection known as the Whiskey Rebellion.

A second reason that Tracy Ridge drew me in was its physical connections to the past. Through my research I found that it had been home and hunting grounds to two of the most well-known Pennsylvania huntsmen of the nineteenth century: Philip Tome and E. N. Woodcock.

Born in southcentral Pennsylvania on March 22, 1782, Philip Tome arrived along the upper Allegheny about 1820. He eventually settled permanently and built a cabin near the mouth of Willow Creek (the stream that marks the northern boundary of FAW's proposed Tracy Ridge Wilderness) in

1827. This location eventually grew into the town of Corydon, which was lost, in turn, to the Kinzua Dam.

A contemporary of Cornplanter – in fact, he acted as the Seneca chief's interpreter on occasion – Tome dabbled in farming and lumbering. His true calling, though, was as a professional hunter and it was for this that he became famous, especially after the 1854 publication of his autobiography, *Pioneer Life; or Thirty Years a Hunter*. Among his many other feats in the woods, Tome was known for capturing live elk and bringing them back unharmed. He did this at least twice in his life, once to settle a bet with Cornplanter.

E.N. Woodcock, Davy Crockett to Tome's pioneering Daniel Boone, was born on August 30, 1844, just a few dozen miles east of Corydon. Following his life's passion, he too became a market hunter and trapper, and eventually published his own woodsman's memoirs as well (the book – with the familiar sounding title *Fifty Years a Hunter and Trapper* – was published in 1941 from a collection of articles written by Woodcock and published in *Hunter-Trader-Trapper* magazine in the early 1900s).

Woodcock hunted this region on several occasions and two chapters of his book are dedicated specifically to the area: "A Hunt on the Kinzua' (Chapter VI) and "My Last Hunt on the Kinzua" (Chapter VII). Although Woodcock never mentions Tome in his book, it's quite likely that he was aware of the earlier woodsman's exploits.

Walking perhaps literally in the footsteps of these hunters from another era, I passed the Tracy Ridge campground, which was shuttered for the season. Other than the small reflective blazes that marked the trails, it was the last sign of human trappings I would encounter that day.

The trail that I followed took me past a huge rock formation, where I stopped for a moment to squeeze a puff of powder into the pan of my rifle. From this point I could gaze out over the valley of Tracy Run, an unbroken expanse of tall hardwood timber and scattered boulders as far down the ridge as I could see.

I thought of the hunters who had come to this valley two centuries before me and faced a forbidding wilderness without the comforting thought of a warm vehicle waiting at the end of the day. By being out here alone today, I was striving to make a thin slice of their experiences my own. It was hard to say whether it was those notions or a passing cloud that caused a chill to rattle its way down my spine.

I hadn't gone more than a couple hundred yards along the Johnnycake Trail when I encountered a set of deer tracks. It looked like a pair of deer had come out of the woods to drink from a puddle in the middle of the trail. With the muddy ground and slushy snow around the puddle, it was difficult to tell whether the tracks had been made this morning or much earlier. Figuring that I still had a lot of ground to cover and would find better opportunities ahead, I passed the tracks by and strode down the trail.

The last of September the deer begin to leave the thickets and move from one place to another, and for several months they are constantly in motion. The hunter has only to station himself near one of their paths, and shoot them as they pass. When the first snows come they can be tracked to the places where herds of them lie at night, and the hunter can keep near a herd and pick them off with his rifle. – Philip Tome.

The trail steepened as it reached the headwaters of Johnnycake Run. Within a few dozen yards, the stream appeared to be running down the trail itself as the sodden earth looked for any route available to rid itself of water. With the snow cushioning my footfalls and the burbling stream camouflaging the sound of any missteps, I found that I couldn't hear myself walking through the woods. On top of that, the wind here in the valley had died entirely. The conditions were exactly perfect for still-hunting.

Less than half an hour passed before I found my next opportunity. Two sets of deer tracks came down the hillside to my right and crossed the Johnnycake Trail. The tracks turned and paralleled the trail for about 20 yards before they veered again to the south and crossed Johnnycake Run. They looked fresh; I doubted they were more than two hours old.

I looked up at the sky, and then gazed at the gray and white forest around me. Well, I thought, this is what you came for. Let's do it.

Almost the entire distance was through the woods and over the rock. There was no sign of a road...On the fourth day we intended to cut wood all day...but before 10 o'clock it began to snow. In a couple of hours there was a good tracking snow and the boys were bound to go out and see if they could not kill a deer. I tried hard to get them to stick to the wood job, but it was no use, they must go hunting. – E.N. Woodcock

Leaping across the narrow stream, I followed the tracks as they meandered along the south bank. The pair of deer did not seem to be in any particular hurry. Their trail occasionally wandered up the sidehill and back down again where a tasty-looking piece of brush must have caught their attention.

I picked my way at an infinitesimal pace, stopping for long stretches to examine the woods around me. My still-hunting method is always the same: take only a few steps at a time, stop frequently for long stretches, and always stop near a tree or boulder for camouflage. It took me several years to learn the technique and the patience required for this method of hunting, but as I've gotten more accustomed to it I've taken several deer, including one of my nicest bucks.

As the tracks worked their way downstream, I found myself looking at a small but thick stand of tall hemlocks ahead. The dense cover of the evergreens made the grove darker than the open oak and cherry woods around it. With a few thick laurel bushes clinging to the hillside, it seemed to me a perfect spot for the deer to have stopped, perhaps even bedding down.

I stopped and studied the hemlock stand carefully for about 15 minutes. I scanned every inch in my sight, looking intently for the outline of a foreleg or the twitch of an ear. I saw nothing but branches and twigs.

I crept slowly into the hemlocks. Moving as stealthily as possible from one trunk to the next, I worked my way through the copse and out the other side. The tracks told the tale: the pair had indeed stopped and milled about in the thicker cover, but then decided to move on, still in no particular hurry. From the condition of the tracks as they left the stand, I knew I had made up some time on them.

The track had been made during the night when it was still snowing...The track led down...in the direction of low hemlocks. I was working my way very carefully thinking that the deer had gone down into those low hemlocks...and were lying down in the thicket. – E.N.W.

A few hundred yards downstream of the hemlock grove, the tracks crossed again to the north side of Johnnycake Run. I picked my way back across the stream, although it was quite a bit wider here and about 18 inches deep.

At this point, the two tracks began to loop around the face of a ridge that jutted out toward Johnnycake Run. They turned up a broad, flat valley that quickly got steeper as I walked up. Within minutes, Johnnycake Run was out of sight. About a half-mile up the hollow the tracks took a sudden turn to the left, crossed the stream and climbed a steep ridge to the northwest.

Following doggedly, I reached the flat crest of the ridge and got two surprises. First, the two deer that I had been following for nearly two hours had bumped into several of their buddies. Their tracks were a mish-mash of milling about, and I had a difficult time discerning the pattern except for the fact that they had left this spot in a hell of a big hurry.

I tromped around for several minutes, stopping to gnaw on some deer jerky that I had stashed in my vest. Walking to the edge of the ridge and looking down, I got my second surprise. I could see my backtrail from here, which meant the deer had watched me walk up the valley below. When they realized I was on their trail, they lit down the backside of the ridge away from my line of sight, covering six feet at a bound.

Realizing that they were now only minutes ahead – and that their number had doubled or possibly tripled – it was hard to maintain the slow pace that the still-hunt demanded. I slipped and skidded down the hillside from the combination of powdery snow and anticipation. At the bottom of the slope was Whisky Run and I stopped for a moment there to get my pace under control and to scan the woods ahead.

From the south side of the stream I could see the trail where the herd of deer had climbed the far bank and ascended the next steep ridge to the north. Convincing my body to go slowly up that hill was easy because the ascent was tortuous. Though the temperature was still in the 20s, I was pouring out sweat like a lawn sprinkler as I lumbered over downed trees and skirted around laurel thickets. The idea that a deer might be standing around each clump of brush seemed to drive my body temperature even higher.

As the tracks neared the top of the ridge, they veered right, staying just below the rim. The deer obviously thought they had rid themselves of the pursuing pest because the tracks were now spaced at a slow walk. They were also no longer moving single file, but meandering side-by-side. I knew that they were close and no longer alarmed.

With the trails diverging, I picked one set of tracks and stuck to them. They paralleled Whisky Run upstream until, at the top of the watershed, the hollow gradually petered out to a laurel-covered flat.

I stopped next to an oak tree to survey the ground ahead. I stood there for two, maybe three minutes, looking across the flat, when the branch that I had stared at three different times suddenly morphed into the head of a doe, standing 60 yards ahead.

Although the deer was looking right at me, I hoped couldn't she pick out my outline against the oak. Slowly, painfully, I eased the rifle up. Although her ears remained alert, she never moved.

Looking down the barrel of the gun, I realized that there was a clump of laurel between us that was going to block my shot. I needed about two steps to my left to get a clear lane. I hesitated, pondering whether I could move without spooking her.

Unfortunately, I never got to find out. At that instant a rogue gust of wind blew up out of Whisky Run behind me. The doe snorted once and was gone. My tired arms let the rifle barrel sag.

Abruptly, the woods around me exploded with running deer. One bounded in from my left, following the doe that I had been watching. I snapped the rifle back up, but saw nothing except her rump as she raced away.

There was a sudden rustling and snapping of twigs on my right. I turned to see the rest of the herd I was trailing, at least eight deer, bolting at a variety of angles into the woods ahead of me. Unfortunately, they were too far away and there was too much brush between them and me. They were gone in seconds without ever presenting a shot.

When he discovered a deer, he slipped down, and endeavored to approach it by another direction than the one in which they were moving, as they always look behind them for danger. It is always necessary for the hunter to keep on the lee-ward side of the deer, as their keen scent will detect his presence and flee, long before he can approach within shot, if the wind blows from him to the deer. – P.T.

Although I was peeved at not getting a shot, I now knew exactly where the deer were. Since it was only midday, I also knew I had plenty of time left to track them down. And that was precisely what I intended to do.

When they bolted from the top of Whisky Run, the deer ran across the Tracy Ridge hiking trail and started down a hollow toward Tracy Run before doubling back to their left. Again, after a few hundred yards the tracks diverged as the deer seemed to settle down. I picked what looked to be the largest set, in hopes that they might belong to a buck, and shifted into stealth mode again.

Eventually this set of tracks drifted back up the hill and followed the Tracy Ridge Trail for a bit. But just before it reached the nose of the ridge, where the trail dives down toward Tracy Run and the Allegheny Reservoir below, the deer took a sudden 180 degree turn. It crossed the narrow, flat top of the ridge and walked along the other face in the opposite direction. I wondered whether this was another deliberate attempt to throw me off the trail.

I was now walking south, with the mountain ridge on my left. I moved as slowly as I could force myself, but it was a constant struggle against my own adrenaline. I knew there were deer in these woods and I could almost sense that they were close.

I was sneaking from one large black oak to another when I glanced down over the slope to my right. I froze. There, grazing among some downed trees, stood two does.

When I first spotted them, the smaller of the two was much closer to the bottom of the hillside, and therefore, to me. As soon as I stopped, she moved toward the larger one. I stood still for a minute or two, worried that I'd spooked them, but the bigger doe kept her head down, eating and pawing the ground nonchalantly.

Although the deer were in sight, they were not in range. They stood at the bottom of a steep hill, nearly a cliff, probably 120 yards away. I had to find a way to close some of that distance if I was going to get a shot.

Without moving, I surveyed the woods around me. Making notes of the size and position of each nearby tree, I mentally mapped out a path that would close the distance while covering my approach.

Crouching, I slipped slowly and carefully from tree to tree. My route took me over the lip of the hill, until I finally reached a point where it was too steep to continue unnoticed. There I hid behind a forked maple tree.

I had the satisfaction of seeing three deer feeding along the hillside and coming in my direction...The wind was in my favor, and as the deer were rather too far to shoot, I stood quiet, only occasionally moving from one tree to another as a favorable opportunity occurred. The deer finally worked up in gun shot, and they proved to be an old doe, a yearling and the doe's fawn. - E.N.W.

Now I had good cover and a clear view of the two does, but it still wasn't going to be an easy shot. They were pretty far away - I guessed the distance to be about 90 yards - and straight downhill. Remembering that shooting downhill would take the round ball lower than intended, I tried to guess how much I would have to compensate.

The smaller doe now began prancing around nervously. The larger one ignored her at first, but then began to move off to the right. Now was the time.

I pulled the long rifle to my shoulder and held the barrel against the right side of the maple to steady it. I was leaning so far downhill that I had a momentary feeling of vertigo, as though I might tumble forward on top of the deer, landing on them headfirst.

Pushing the sensation aside, I took aim at the bigger doe. I lined up the sights on her ribcage, and then, to adjust for the angle, slowly slid the barrel up until the sights rested just above the top of her back.

The sequence was automatic. Ease back the hammer. Feel it lock. Draw back the set trigger. Feel it click. Hold on the aiming point.

Fire.

Through the cloud of smoke that curled from the rifle, I could see both deer jump and run off to the right. I knew I hadn't flinched, but with the distance and elevation, I had no idea whether I had hit her.

I hadn't. A quick check of the area showed no blood on the snow, and a more thorough investigation showed me why.

Lining up the tree I had shot from and the spot where the doe had stood, I pinpointed the flight of my roundball. And there, about a foot and a half behind her tracks in the snow was the mark where the ball had hit the ground. I had shot directly over her back, probably by no more than an inch or two.

From my trip down the hill I already knew the reason why the shot was high. Fooled by the steep slope, I had guessed the distance to be 90 yards when it was much closer to 70. At the shorter distance, the roundball had gone exactly where I aimed it, right over her back.

After working so hard for over three hours to get a shot, it was disappointing to miss. But given the conditions, I knew that was going to be a tough shot. Plus, I took solace in the fact that I still had about four more hours of daylight and tracks as clear as a roadmap to lead me back to the deer.

...I climbed the ridge to look for deer and got two shots during the afternoon but missed both. All came to camp that night without killing any deer. – E.N.W.

After my shot, the two does eventually swung west toward the Allegheny Reservoir, and then south along the steep ledge that overlooks the reservoir. Here they joined again with a larger group of deer. Moving at a quicker pace now, the herd re-crossed Whisky Run, then Johnnycake Run as they continued south.

I stayed locked on their trail until I came to Johnnycake Run, where the water depth caused me to retreat upstream to find a better crossing point. It took me nearly twenty minutes get back to their tracks on the other side, and when I did, the herd threw me a curve that nearly got me off their tails for good.

For the fourth time since I started tracking them, the deer started one direction – in this case, upstream along Johnnycake Run – then reversed their course. By now I had decided that this had to be a deliberate effort to get rid of me. This time it almost worked for two reasons: first, instead of making a looping turn as they had before, the deer doubled back on top of their own tracks; second, they happened to do it in an open area of the woods where the afternoon sunshine had softened the snow, making the trail much harder to read.

I lost nearly 45 minutes pacing back and forth, staring down at the snow, until I finally deduced their correct course. They had turned back downstream, paralleling Johnnycake Run.

I knew now that time was against me, so I picked up my pace. I needed to close the gap on these deer so I abandoned my usual still-hunt strategy and once I was sure there were no deer in sight, I hustled through every open piece of woods.

Clambering up and down steep ridges and crossing one small stream after another, I walked for miles along the eastern rim of the reservoir. The deer seemed to be avoiding the tops of the ridges, preferring instead to wrap their trail along the hillsides, following the sinuous landscape.

At last, in an area of tall hemlocks and broken topography, I caught up with them. I knew from the condition of the tracks that I had been gaining on them, but I was still surprised as I climbed on all fours up a rocky ledge and peeked over the top to see four does looking back at me from 60 yards away.

I had to climb a few feet more before I could get footing solid enough to even raise my rifle. As I did, the deer started to move.

They weren't running, but as I tried to draw a bead they seemed to disappear and reappear every few seconds amid the checkerboard pattern of hemlocks. Once again, there was no chance for a shot.

I was making good time when on looking ahead along the ridge I saw a good-sized buck come from the left hand side of the ridge. He would take a jump or two then drop his head to the ground. I knew that he was on the trail of other deer. I had hardly time to bring my gun to my shoulder when the buck wheeled and disappeared back over the ridge from where he had come. – E.N.W.

The deer plunged down the hollow to my right, once again doubling back on their course. With less than two hours of daylight left, I took off in hot pursuit. They ran almost exactly parallel to their path of the last hour or so, except slightly further down the ridge. I stayed on the track, but with frequent nervous glances at the sun as it worked its way over my left shoulder.

When the tracks once again approached Johnnycake Run, they veered upstream. My first reaction was relief because I knew there was no way I could follow them if they crossed the swollen stream at this point. But as the tracks continued on a straight line upstream, my heart began to sink. I knew what was going to happen.

Sure enough, the number of tracks in the snow suddenly doubled as the deer retraced their steps from two hours before – at the very spot where they had nearly thrown me off once already.

I looked at the dipping sun and then at my watch. It was 4:15 PM. At most, I had an hour of daylight left and I was at least three miles from my truck, not to mention about 800 feet lower in elevation.

Remembering that it had taken me the better part of an hour to sort out these tracks once before, I knew that time had run out on my backcountry hunt. The deer had gotten away.

I slowly started my trek back up the valley of Johnnycake Run. In the instant that I decided to quit the pursuit, it seemed that a massive load had fallen onto my body.

My upper back, already sore when I awoke this morning, now burned and twitched in spasms from eight hours of carrying the heavy Pennsylvania rifle. My legs suddenly felt wobbly and weak, and I realized that I hadn't sat down since I left the truck. Mapping my route on a topographic map later, I calculated that I had walked over 16 miles on my Tracy Ridge hunt.

Despite my sudden exhaustion and the fact that, for all my exertions, I hadn't been able to bring down a deer, I felt my spirits rise as I marched out of the valley. I thought of my excitement as I cut the pair of deer tracks in the morning and of the building anticipation as the tracks became clearer and fresher during my pursuit.

I reflected on my woodsman's skills as I reeled those deer in, enabling me to get one shot and two other opportunities for shots, even though the deer knew I was trailing them. I gazed around at the gorgeous forest of Tracy Ridge – stout oaks, gray-barked maples, thick cherries trees, and towering hemlocks with their branches still painted by the icy dust of last night's snowfall. It was one of the most gorgeous venues that I had ever hunted.

When it occurred to me that I had not seen so much as a footprint from another human, I realized that my wilderness muzzleloader hunt had been a success. As I reached the head of Johnnycake Run, I turned back and looked out over the sweeping valley below. It came to me that my expectation for the day had not really been to take a deer at all – although that would have been a perfect ending. What I really wanted was to use an old-fashioned gun and old-fashioned hunting techniques to stalk through a wilderness and match my skills against those of a truly wild animal.

Staring into the gathering gloom of the early winter evening, I knew that this expectation had been met in nearly every way I could have hoped. It ranked as one of the most satisfying days that I had ever spent afield.

I laid the rifle over my shoulder and turned toward the truck. I wasn't too tired to smile.

Every hunter of long experience could tell of the ups and downs along the trail consisting of good, bad and indifferent luck and as usual tell of our hits and let others tell of our misses...– E.N.W.

CHAPTER 14
SHADES OF GRAY

Just like so many other American hunters, my first quarry as a youngster was the gray squirrel. When I close my eyes, I can still picture that first one hopping up onto a moss-covered log as I stared down the barrel of my 20-gauge at him. Perhaps because of the success of that first day – and many more like it since – chasing these manic tree-dwellers has always represented in my mind one of the greatest simple pleasures of hunting.

As for my Allegheny adventure, the days were getting longer, but the hunting seasons were getting shorter as January came to a close. There was time for just one more hunt this winter and gray squirrels would be the prey.

As I found out in deer and bear seasons, the mast crop on the Forest this year had been a complete failure. That fact, combined with the 10-plus inches of snow and sub-zero temperatures that the first week of February had brought to the Allegheny, was going to make finding bushytails a challenge. Still, with the morning dawning as clear and icy as mountain spring water, my mood climbed as I drove north.

It stayed that way until I neared the Allegheny, when a radio news report broke my cheerful spell. During a rundown of year-end statistics, the newsman reported in a dire tone that the National Forest counties of Elk, McKean, and Warren had all posted unemployment rates between six and seven percent for the past year, far above the statewide rate of just 5.4 percent. Forest County, which has a much higher percentage of National Forest land than the other three, had an unemployment rate more than double the statewide level, a staggering 13 percent.

I was shocked. I knew from my research that the communities around the Allegheny had been struggling financially, but with all of the optimistic talk I'd heard about a shift to a greener recreation and tourism based economy, I thought things were rebounding. Clearly not.

The sad irony is that during the Big Timber era of the late nineteenth century, this region had one of the largest concentrations of wealth in the robust young nation. And later, the Allegheny's recovery from intensive logging coincided perfectly with the era of the traveling hunter – a concept made possible by the simultaneous advent of the automobile and an increase in leisure time. This confluence allowed the development of a thriving economy for hotels, restaurants, and sporting goods stores that revolved around the annual migration of hunters to the federal land near the northwest corner of the state.

"Back in the day, you literally could not find a place to park in Ridgway starting the Friday after Thanksgiving," says Bob Imhof, a local economic development expert. Bob, brother of Clarion River historian John Imhof, explains that, "Back then, people used to rent rooms to hunters right in their homes. They cooked meals for them, the hunters stayed in town, and it generated income for the local people."

Nationwide, outdoorsmen and women are indisputably an economic force to be reckoned with today. By one estimate, the folks who crowd the woods and waterways each weekend could fill every NFL and Major League Baseball stadium, along with every NASCAR venue, six times over. If their combined economic contribution were magically brought into one company, it would create a $70 billion corporation – the 11th largest in America. Hunters alone spend more than $4.6 billion on specialty gear annually, including $605 million just on their dogs.[64] Hunter wishes he had it so good.

In Pennsylvania, with one of the highest hunter populations in the nation, the sport also makes a monstrous economic contribution. Statewide, roughly $1.2 billion in annual hunting gear sales supports over 19,000 jobs for employees who earn over $500 million in wages.

Why then, with outdoor expenditures reaching all-time highs, is the Allegheny, one of the premier outdoor venues in the East and a destination located within a day's drive of more than half of the US population, lagging economically?

Like any economic question, there is no simple answer. Part of the equation is Bucktail Hotel owner Barbara Kuhl's observation that hunters – not to mention anglers, ATV riders, hikers, and all other outdoor adventurers – are more self-contained today. In an effort to save money they buy food, gas, and other supplies before leaving home rather than frequenting local establishments near the Allegheny.

Bob Imhof agrees that this is a major factor. "It's not half what it used to be," he says of spending by hunters on the Allegheny. "They bought camps and became more self-sufficient when they're up here. They became less dependent on the community itself."

Land use changes have also had an effect. Especially when it comes to deer hunting, many areas that once took a back seat to the Allegheny have caught up and blown right by. I remember clearly the words of Sean Riley as we sat around the table at Camp Stockert one evening: "I don't come up here just to get a buck. If I wanted to do that I would hunt around home because there're a lot bigger bucks down there. I come to see everyone at camp, to sit around like this and talk, and to enjoy myself. That's the main reason why I come up here." Each year, though, more hunters choose the quality deer hunting near home over that long trip to the Allegheny.

Social changes and the overall decline in the number of hunters have also contributed to the declining economic impact. As Elk County Commissioner Dan Freeburg told me, "Up through the '60s and '70s, hunting season made [the business owner's] year financially. But now, there has been a huge change in family dynamics. It used to be the father and grandfather taking the kid hunting – that was just the way it was – but it doesn't happen anymore."

While acknowledging that the maturing timber on the National Forest has driven many hunters to "farm country" to chase deer, Freeburg adds, "It's so much bigger than the physical characteristics of the forest. Hunting is just not anywhere near as strong as it used to be." Perhaps if just a few more kids could sense the thrill of looking down the shiny barrel of a shotgun at a jittery gray squirrel...

Of course, a decline in hunting is not the only source of economic distress around the Allegheny. Traditional employers like the timber industry have weakened – partly because of the lawsuit-driven logging moratorium on the National Forest – and the much-touted recreation economy has not expanded to fill the gaps. On top of that, land use restrictions in and near the Forest work against those with a development vision.

"It restricts the potential development space adjacent to communities," Bob Imhof says. "It's wonderful to have [the Forest] for its beauty and environment, but sometimes having a federal landholding in your backyard – you wonder if it's worth it. All the lawsuits and regulations have contributed to keeping economic development stagnant and communities can't physically expand even where there is the potential for development."

My own lifelong connection to the Allegheny, renewed and strengthened by my recent adventures, kindled a desire to roll up my sleeves and pitch in. But where to begin?

Even as an outsider, I could sense the frustration of those who are straining to bring in each dollar to their community. As Bob suggests, I've seen development plans nixed because government-owned land could not be acquired. At the same time, I've encountered entrepreneurs who were forced to shutter their businesses because the very rustic nature that attracted them eventually squeezed them dry, either from a lack of utility infrastructure, poor road access, or simply too few customers through the door.

This frustration has resulted in a sort of homegrown malaise. Feeling bound by limitations imposed by a distant federal government, and too poor or too detached to generate the type of meaningful local investment that would have tangible economic benefits, many have resigned themselves to simply plodding along, hoping for more but settling for less.

Feeling some of this same irritation at not knowing where or how to help, I resolved to start small. I would make at least a token economic contribution by stopping in town for a bite to eat before I left today. First, though, I had squirrels to hunt.

The destination for the hunt was the Laurel Mill recreation area just west of Ridgway, near the very southeastern corner of the Allegheny. Dominated by mature oaks, with a few beech and cherries mixed in, it was as good a spot as any in this weak mast year.

When I pulled into the parking lot at about 7:45 AM, there were already a couple of other cars there. The roof racks told me that they belonged to folks who were using the cross-country ski trail here at Laurel Mill. With safety in mind, I set out in the opposite direction.

I had considered using my single-shot Winchester .22 for today's hunt, and even thought briefly of taking out the Pennsylvania rifle, which I've used to bag squirrels in the past. But when I looked in the gun cabinet that morning the old Crescent side by side caught my eye and so, for no special reason, that was the gun I carried into the woods.

A blanket of snow covered the entire woods, occasionally spilling over the tops of my 10-inch felt pack boots. With that kind of snow cover and a lack of acorns on the ground anyway, I knew that my normal strategy of simply camping out near a supply of nuts and waiting for the squirrels to arrive wasn't going to cut it today. Instead, I tried to make the snow work to my advantage by still-hunting. I would walk until I found a set of tracks then follow them to a live animal.

The first set of tracks I found was just a few yards into the woods, which was certainly an encouraging sign. I decided that they were too close to the parking lot for safe shooting, however, so I passed them by and moved deeper into the forest. Despite my high hopes, I soon discovered that this first set of tracks had been an aberration – I walked over a mile before I found the next set.

Studying the trail ahead of me, I could tell that the squirrel had bounced between two smallish cherry trees. As I walked over to one of the cherries to get a closer look, a spark of movement caught my eye.

For a few seconds, I couldn't pick out the source. Then, against the trunk of a cherry tree about 25 yards away, I caught the slight twitch of a tail and the squirrel's body suddenly materialized.

It was an easy shot. He was trying to be invisible, frozen against the tree trunk with his head up and his back facing me. I drew up the 12-gauge, lined up the bead, and fired. Then I watched in amazement as the fat gray rodent bounded away across the top of the snow.

I walked about three-quarters of the distance to where he had been when I found the source of my miss. A two-inch maple sapling that I had somehow failed to notice had taken the brunt of my load, allowing only a few scattered pellets to reach the target. There was not a drop of blood in the snow.

I had seen the squirrel scamper up into a three-forked oak tree, so I had the luxury of laughing at myself without feeling too bad about it. I moved off about 25 yards from the oak and sat on a downed log. I waited for him to make the next move.

When a half-hour passed with no action, I began to wonder whether I had picked out the right tree to watch. I decided to get a closer look and got up to check his tracks.

As I thought, they ended at the split oak. I walked closer to try to see whether the squirrel might be hiding on the back of one of the trunks. When I reached the tree, I leaned my head close and stared upward.

Suddenly, something stirred in the base of the split, just above my eye level. I jumped back before realizing that it was the squirrel, who had tucked himself down in the crotch of the tree.

He was close enough that I could have whacked him on the head with my shotgun barrel. Sensing this, he dashed up the trunk to safer quarters.

Now the game was on. He swung from one side of the trunk to the other then leapt to yet another trunk as I waltzed around the base of the tree, squinting into the blue sky, trying for a clear shot. It took a concerted effort at one point to keep from laughing out loud.

Inevitably, the squirrel dodged the wrong direction. I fired and he helicoptered down from about 30 feet up, close enough that, had I taken two quick steps, I could have caught him in my gloved hand.

The snow was so deep that only the very tip of his bushy tail was visible poking up out. I reached down and grasped that tail, lifting him out of his snowy grave.

Despite the lack of food around the Forest, this gray was hefty and long. Bits of icy snow clung to his silvery coat as I turned him over in my hand.

As I tucked him into my game bag, it dawned on me that, though we tend to separate and specialize – bird hunters versus rabbit hunters, turkey hunters versus deer hunters, bowhunters versus rifle hunters – the essence of the chase changes little. At that moment, I was as thrilled as if I had downed a pheasant or dropped a goose as it came into the blind.

I hoped that this would be the first of a bagful of squirrels on the day, but that was not to be. I hunted for another four hours, finding only two more sets of fresh tracks. I staked each out patiently, but neither led to another squirrel. It was simply too cold, with too much snow and not enough food for the grays to be moving, other than the unlucky old boy I was carrying home.

Before going home, I followed through on my pledge to stop and have a sit-down meal in Ridgway. Parking on the main drag, I picked the Ridgway Grill – mainly by virtue of its being the only place that seemed open on a Saturday afternoon – and strode through the heavy wooden door to grab a bite.

Other than the stuffed coyote and turkey above the bar, the Ridgway Grill could have been the Anywhere Grill. Its ordinary collection of neon beer sign and posters of barely-clad women did little to distinguish it from a hundred other bars. Still, the price was right. A bacon cheeseburger, fries, bowl of chili, and a cold draft only set me back $8.50.

I was itching to get some local flavor on the National Forest so I tried to strike up a conversation with the bartender, and then the guy next to me. But they were more interested in the two loudmouths at the end of the bar who were arguing over a presidential race that had been decided three months before. It was, I thought glumly, a fitting metaphor for the country as a whole.

Then again, maybe it was just one more symptom of the melancholy that seems to pervade the local population here, an attitude that isn't so surprising when your backyard is a constant, swirling battlefield of complaints, demonstrations, and lawsuits.

"That block of land represents the old, 100-year-ago cut land that no one felt was worth anything," says Elk County Commissioner Freeburg. "But when it became new forest it became valuable again. What it typifies now is the struggle: the old, which is [timber] cutting only, and the new, which is multi-use. The industry people aren't wrong in saying that cutting is needed for improving forest health, but the naturalists are saying that it needs to be protected, which is not wrong either."

"It's a great resource to have on our back door," he continues forcefully. "There's a big green block on the national map. That alone can make it a new opportunity for economic stimulus. There just can't be these extreme left and right uses fighting. The fighting has just shut down everyone and now no one's winning." His solution is simple: "Let there be a place for everyone."

Doug Carlson, Executive Director of the Conservation District Planning Department for Forest County, doesn't share Freeburg's stance in the middle of the road. Carlson feels that the Allegheny National Forest has become a conduit for outside interests to get their way at the expense of local residents. "Where Federal ownership occurs," he states, "local people suffer impacts that are unjust, yet are justified, with the phrase 'societal good.' Rural citizens and rural lifestyles are fast becoming the newest endangered species."[65]

Clearly there are tough societal and economic challenges that fall onto the communities around the Allegheny. The fact that there are no easy answers is even more apparent.

Or is it? Is the answer as simple as everyone giving up their iron-gripped position and moving toward a more stable and beneficial middle ground? When listening to Freeburg, I start to be convinced that this straightforward solution might work.

"Rural ideologies resist change," he told me. "We're moving from an industrial to a modern economy not totally based in resource extraction. [The Allegheny] should be a land of opportunity, not a negative force. We have to balance recreation with timber demands. It's a complicated network, but I know it can happen.

"Look at the Clarion River; it's a perfect example. That river was a black, stinking mess in the '70s and early '80s. My father was a big time fisherman and fished the Clarion tributaries and he'd have to scrub his waders after he crossed the Clarion because the water was so filthy. And now today it's a great fishery and it's full of canoes every weekend. This cleanup has really been recent. The awesome power that nature has can heal what man does. And people who don't know the forest have to understand that the same is true when you cut timber. It's needed and it helps the economy, and the impact on the forest is not permanent. They need to understand that. They need to know that there's room for everyone."

Weeks after my squirrel hunt, I twisted that over in my mind. A half-a-million acre is an awful lot of space.

Then I remembered returning to my truck on that snowy morning at Laurel Mill. In the parking space next to me a young mom was changing her toddler son's clothes after a morning of sled riding along the ski trail. We briefly struck up a conversation and when I stooped to help lift some equipment out of the back of her Saab wagon, I was hit by the incongruity of their pastel-colored down jackets against the safety orange of my hunting vest. At the same time, I was impressed that she didn't shy away from me, even while I was stowing my shotgun in its case on the tailgate of the truck.

Maybe there is room for everyone on the Allegheny. And maybe her son will someday sit silently in the woods, holding his breath as a gray squirrel hops within range.

For his sake and the sake of his community, I hope so.

CHAPTER 15

SPRING AHEAD, LOOK BACK

I read recently that 64 percent of hunters claim they don't get out in the field as often as they would like. Something about that number seems wrong to me.

It's much too low. Frankly, I can't envision even one of my hunting buddies saying, "I don't think I'm going to go out today. I feel like I've hunted enough already."

In that same survey, most hunters listed either 'Not enough time' or 'Work and family obligations' as the reasons they didn't hunt often enough. They said they were sitting at their desks, or driving the kids from one sporting event to another, or preparing to host a party with a houseful of guests instead of plucking a hickory stick across a slate and ogling a gobbler with a beard dangling so low that it scrapes the tops of the new spring grass.

OK, I made that last part up.

But that was the angst I felt when the last few hours of the spring turkey season were ticking away and I had not taken so much as a Sunday drive through the Allegheny National Forest. Taunted nearly every morning by the fat, cocky gobblers that frequent the fields around my home, my daily commute was tortuous.

And the few days that I didn't have to be in the office, I alternated with Pam as we drove Rachel to track practice or Stephanie to softball games. Throw in time spent prepping for Rachel's twelfth birthday party and, well, you get the idea.

In the blink of a firefly, the end of the season, Memorial Day weekend, was upon me. Reluctant to let it slide by without even a token effort, I called Dan Brophy to take him up on his leftover turkey hunting offer from last fall. Our schedules were so hectic that we found ourselves communicating via serial voice mail instead of person to person.

His recordings told me he hadn't gotten a gobbler on the first day of the spring season, and hadn't had a chance to get back out since then. Like me, he was anxious to remedy that situation. We narrowed our options down to either Tuesday or Wednesday of the final week when commitments and obligations suddenly – and tragically – intervened once again.

Half a world away, Sgt. Carl Morgain, a 40-year old National Guardsman from Butler, Pennsylvania, was killed by a car bomb at a security checkpoint in Iraq. Because Dan had volunteered to be part of the funeral guard, and Morgain's body was returning to the States in time for Memorial Day, Dan's week would be taken up with drilling and funeral services. Due to far greater priorities, our turkey trip was off.

With that my chances for a spring gobbler hunt dwindled to almost nil. I had a series of unavoidable meetings that would consume the rest of my week, leaving me with only Saturday, which was Rachel's birthday. I talked it over with Pam and Rachel, and since we were holding her party on Sunday, they were willing to concede a few hours on Saturday – as long as I was back in time to help with the last minute preparations. Since Pennsylvania's spring gobbler season only allows hunting until noon, it was an easy promise to make.

With work tying me up until late Friday afternoon, this was going to be a hit-and-run event. I didn't have Camp Brophy to hunt from, and for the sake of time savings I dispensed with the idea of tent camping too. For this no-frills hunt, the front seat of the truck would have to do.

I packed the F-150 for one last trip north, and then stuck around long enough to help Pam tuck the kids into bed. With a round of good luck kisses from each of them, I aimed the truck into the night. The route was familiar now and as usual, I passed it searching for something decent on the radio and daydreaming, succeeding much more at the latter than the former.

As the woolgathering commenced, the first thing that struck me was the symmetry of my Allegheny adventure. My first trip last fall, for early season geese, was on the Friday before Labor Day and now my last trip was on the Friday before Memorial Day. It had a certain balance to it, an evenness that appealed to my sense of proportion.

Like that first trip north nine months ago, I-80 was once again loaded with vehicles, many of which exited toward the Allegheny National Forest. I grinned to myself when I noticed that nearly every vehicle was either a truck or an SUV, a constant theme here in northwestern Pennsylvania. It reminded me of a late night trip to Camp Stockert when I pulled up behind an SUV with a deer carrier attached and a decal showing a massive buck in the back window. The vehicle's Pennsylvania license plate read: "HNT FSH."

The spot I picked for my last minute turkey hunt was on a quiet section of the Forest near Marienville, a place where I had seen turkeys on at least two earlier occasions. Without fanfare, I rolled the Ford to a stop, turned off the ignition, and tried to somehow stuff my 6'2" frame comfortably into the pickup's 5'6" front seat. I hadn't bothered packing a sleeping bag, bringing along just a pillow to ease the suffering slightly. As the overnight temperature plunged into the forties, the extra sweatshirt wrapped around my knees left me somewhat less than toasty.

Cold, cramped, and none too rested, I wasn't terribly upset when my watch alarm beeped loudly at 4 AM. I quickly changed into my camouflage gear and stuffed my pockets with a slate call and a handful of shells. Grabbing a flashlight and the old Crescent side by side one more time, I was into the woods by 4:45.

I slipped noiselessly down the trail, with the branches of the forest reaching out to brush my sleeves in greeting. It was slightly less than a mile to the spot I was looking for – a grassy opening filled with crabapple trees, planted as part of a cooperative habitat project by the NWTF. I hoped that the line of pines to the west might serve as a roost site for a flock of hungry turkeys looking for a morning snack. Not wanting to disturb them, I selected a stand on the side across the field from the pine trees.

I sat with my back propped comfortably in the crook of an old, bent maple tree. The stand was ideal, with a clear view of the opening in three directions. I settled in snugly and watched as the rising sun tinted the morning clouds a glowing rose.

As I waited for dawn and the opportunity to start working the slate, I realized that this was going to be the last day of my season on the Allegheny. It was a bittersweet thought.

On one hand, I was glad that the pressure of the effort was over and I could now pick hunting destinations by my own criteria rather than their ability to tell a story. But on the other hand, the past nine months had provided me with hunting opportunities and enjoyable moments the equal of any in my 25-plus years in the outdoors.

Further, they had allowed me insights into the workings of a half-million acre piece of public land as remarkable and unique in its history and ecology as any in the country. The experiences and understanding that had come from this effort were irreplaceable.

As I ruminated, it also occurred to me that there would be far fewer trips to the Allegheny next year. Sure, I had earned invites back to Camp Brophy and Camp Stockert, but I knew my time demands were going to be quite different a season from now. And the biggest change of all was actually occurring today, as I sat waiting for the sun to rise and turkeys to fly down.

Rachel was turning 12 today, legal hunting age in Pennsylvania, which meant she would be coming along on most of my hunts well into the foreseeable future. With Stephanie only three years behind her, and Jake three years behind that, my days of solo hunting, if not gone entirely, would at least be severely curtailed for the next decade or so.

I can barely wait to take them on their first Youth Pheasant Hunts, possibly at the Beanfield. My heart is already turning to mush at the thought of hugging Stephanie as she stands over her first buck or seeing Rachel take her first grouse from Hunter's sleek, gray jaws. But I also recognize that this will be a permanent change from the way I have hunted for more than two decades. There will be no more long, solitary Saturday hunts or days afield with just the dog and me. It's hard enough to convince the kids to stay behind now; with a license pinned to the back of their vests, I'm certain it will be impossible.

My reflective train of thought was soon derailed by the realization that the dawn was upon me. I slid the call slowly into my lap and rasped out a series of clucks and putts. With no response after 10 minutes, I let loose another round.

The only reply came from a flock of geese winging by on the morning breeze. Their raucous honking as they passed overhead made me wonder if they were headed to the propagation area at Buzzard Swamp, habitually seeking safety in its comfortable embrace.

The thought of geese and ducks also drew me back to my Clarion River duck hunt with Dan Fitzgerald. I grinned behind my camo facemask when I thought of our night at the Hallton Hilton, the drunken blonde who earned a permanent spot in our hunting lore, and our unexpected dip in the river the next day. That had been quite a trip all the way around and I smiled again as I wondered whether Fitzgerald would ever consent to another duck hunt with me.

I hit the turkey call every 15 minutes or so for the first 90 minutes of the morning, but had no response at all. As had happened so many times while I hunted the Allegheny, the clouds were thickening above. The woods around me seemed to pull within themselves in anticipation of the coming rain; the wind was silent and not even a songbird moved among the tree branches.

With the nasty weather closing in I knew I needed to make something happen, so I abandoned my spot and deeper into the woods. As I walked along I spied what appeared to be a grassy clearing in the middle of the woods. Cresting a small knoll, I peeked into the glade. Rectangular in shape and planted in grass and legumes, it was obviously another habitat area created specifically for turkeys.

Taking care to hide from any birds that might already be lurking in the clearing, I crept stealthily through the saplings along its edge until I found a rest against a dirt mound beneath the spreading branches of an ash tree. Peering over the top of the mound, I saw that the clearing was empty so I took a few minutes to arrange myself comfortably in my new lair before I started calling again.

As I settled in, I noticed crushed weeds and snipped branches that created perfect sight lines into the clearing. Obviously I wasn't the first hunter to hunker here.

Encouraged that someone had taken the time and effort to set this spot up just right, I figured they must have known there were turkeys here. I started working the slate with renewed eagerness and as I waited for a return call, I looked out over the little field and wondered if this too was an NWTF supported project. The question reminded me of a heartwarming story of conservation and caring that I had recently heard from Dave Burdge, president of the Pennsylvania Chapter of NWTF.

Burdge put me in touch with Carol Kostelnik, a spry and humorous retiree from Buffalo, New York. Carol's husband, Leonard Kostelnik Sr., established their connection to the Allegheny in 1956 when he bought 2 ½ acres of land on Whig Hill in Forest County to build a camp. From that point on, Carol told me, "He hunted turkeys, deer, everything down there."

Hunting wildlife was not the only thing Len was passionate about; feeding it was at least as important to him. "There's 500 apple trees all around Forest County that he planted," Carol said with a laugh. "He grew them here at home, and then planted them down there. It cost me more money for food to feed the animals than it did to feed our kids." Then, a bit more quietly, she added, "He was a real conservationist, that I can tell you."

Carol and Len had been married for 46 years, when, at 72 years old, he died suddenly on January 22, 2005. "He was my life," she said, her voice suddenly husky.

When Len passed, Carol and her son and two daughters – Leonard Jr., Barbara, and Elaine – sat down to discuss how to handle memorial donations. With Len having survived both open-heart surgery and cancer, they debated over whether the money from family and friends should be directed to the American Heart Association or the American Cancer Society.

At some point in the conversation, the kids struck on an alternate idea: directing donations to the NWTF for the creation of a food plot in Len's memory. It was the perfect solution. The money would go to the animals that he loved, it would be spent in Forest County (a stipulation that the family insisted upon), and, most importantly, it would feed the animals of the Allegheny.

In total, $2,325 in donations was raised. "Everybody knows that he was an avid turkey hunter," says Carol, "and everybody was very generous."

NWTF contacted the Forest Service and the deal was done. It would be used to create a three-acre food plot, with the money going toward disking, seeding, and "whatever else they could do with that much money," said Carol.

The wildlife food plot on the Allegheny will be a fitting and lasting tribute, not only to Len, but the entire Kostelnik family. Carol, a native of the Warren/Sheffield area, told me, "We spent a lot of time down there over the years. When he retired 15 years ago he spent all his time down there and when I retired four years ago we'd spend all summer together there." She added that she often went along on Len's turkey hunts – carrying a camera instead of a shotgun – and that their kids helped him plant a lot of those 500 apple trees.

While organizations like NWTF, with 500,000 members and millions in annual donations, put something of a corporate face on conservation fundraising, stories like the Kostelniks' remind us that it's the individual contributions of money and time that make those huge numbers possible. Whether it's a $20 membership or a $2,000 remembrance, the fact remains that it's conservation-minded individuals, not the organizations themselves, that create and restore wildlife habitat.

Looking out over the created turkey habitat that I had all to myself on this dank morning, I waited in vain for a lovesick gobbler to answer my calls. I hit the call again, but the only reply came from another flock of geese passing above. Their fading honks took me back to the flocks of snow geese that had flown over during bear season, the first ones I had ever seen here in western Pennsylvania.

I really liked the looks of the little field in the middle of the forest, so I stayed for over an hour, calling intermittently. But the long lack of action eventually convinced me that it was going to last so, with the sky darkening still more, I moved further down the trail.

A half-mile deeper into the forest I found another created opening, this one carpeted in cool season grasses. It was much smaller than the first, only about a quarter-acre in size. I crossed to the far side of the clearing and found that the ground here fell away into the headwaters of a small stream. Thinking that a gobbler might be lurking among the grapevines further down the valley, I picked a spot between the head of the stream and the clearing, then plopped down with my back against a boulder the size of a VW Beetle.

I immediately set to calling, making the slate sing as loudly as I could. A flicker of movement to my right caught my attention, but I quickly realized it was just a red-headed woodpecker working its way through the woods. A few minutes later I heard the cackling call of its larger cousin, the pileated woodpecker, followed by the sound of its bill jackhammering against the trunk of a tree. The two woodpecker sightings brought my drifting mind around to the recent rediscovery of the ivory-billed woodpecker.

These beautiful birds, which were thought to be extinct for over 60 years, have been found once again within the 46,000-acre Cache River National Wildlife Refuge in Arkansas. Their home range today is an area that has been the subject of several habitat conservation projects by duck hunters, who contributed mightily to establishing the refuge within the bottomland hardwood forest of the Cache.

What's more, three-quarters of the refuge land was acquired through funds from the Federal Duck Stamp program, which is supported largely by hunters. As Ducks Unlimited Executive Vice-President Don Young said, "We have an opportunity now to ensure that those forests are conserved and restored not only for the ivory-billed woodpecker, but for...ducks and other waterfowl."

From historic incidents like the woodpecker's reemergence to the impressive effect of habitat work I had seen here on the Allegheny, I was thankful for the actions of hunter-based conservation groups like DU, NWTF, PF, and RGS. The fact that they are carrying on the conservation ethic initiated over a century ago by pioneers like Teddy Roosevelt and Gifford Pinchot, and refined a generation later by Forest Service employees like Aldo Leopold, gave me confidence in the future of our sport and our environment. Their presence helps ensure that the brutal pillaging that first drove Roosevelt and Pinchot to establish National Forests will never be known in our country again.

The assurance that these groups will continue to advocate the sensible disbursement of our cherished resources while actively improving habitat made me more confident that my children – and someday, grandchildren – would enjoy an outdoor world at least as good as the one in which I now sat. Further, I hoped that the sermons my kids had heard from me, as well as the lessons they had taken in from the natural world around them, would persuade them to put their own conservation ethic into action.

Unfortunately, all the habitat improvement in this particular section of the National Forest wasn't helping me one bit today. I hadn't seen or heard a turkey and after 45 minutes at this spot, drops of rain began to pelt the fresh, green leaves.

That sound brought back memories of too many days this year on the Allegheny: the miserably damp turkey hunt with Dan Brophy, the Beanfield pheasant hunt abbreviated by a sudden downpour, and most of all, the drenching torrent that perfectly capped my wretched muzzleloader hunt in the Tionesta virgin forest. I guess I hadn't hunted alone as much as I thought; the rain had been my near-constant companion.

Convinced I was out of luck at this location, I lifted myself stiffly away from the boulder and walked back out to the trail. But rather than bolting directly for the truck as the downpour increased, I defiantly turned the other way and went a bit further into the woods. I wanted to absorb just a little bit more of the Allegheny before my adventure ended.

I had only gone a quarter-mile further when the rain intensified again and I was soon soaking up much more than I wanted. I stopped and gave a couple of half-hearted clucks with the slate call, but it was only a token effort.

I knew I was beaten. Finally, water dripping off the bill of my cap and rolling across my lips and chin, I took one last look around the sodden woods then wheeled and headed back toward the truck.

As I hustled back along the trail, the thought occurred to me that I was once again leaving the Forest empty-handed. There had been a few of those days over the past nine months. The early season goose, snowshoe hare, and pheasant hunts, along with the muzzleloader hunt at Tracy Ridge had all ended with no game to show for my efforts. In fact, on some hunts I never so much as pulled my gun to my shoulder.

But it dawned on me that just because I left the Forest with an empty game bag didn't mean I wasn't taking something home. What I had harvested was a whole new collection of memories.

I recalled camping at Buzzard Swamp on a night so painfully clear that I awoke with a start at 3 AM, convinced by the stark moonlight beaming through the tent that I had overslept and was looking up at the morning sun. And then there was Hunter dashing across a fern-covered glen, with Mark Banker's grouse clasped firmly between his jaws with the bird's brown wing curled over his silky, gray muzzle.

Those moments, and a hundred others, were sometimes a source of inspiration. I was moved by the dedication of people like Mary Hosmer and PF's John Mack, both of whom wear their love of the Forest and their desire to make it better like a badge of honor. Or people like Ken Stockert – who was just as thrilled to help me kill a deer as to bag his own – and Dan Brophy, whose passion for the Allegheny and for his nation are exceeded only by his love for his family.

Then there were days when the Allegheny itself provided inspiration, as it did during my all-day trek on the trail of deer at Tracy Ridge. That adventure stirred thoughts of hunts from two centuries ago, creating one of the best days I have ever spent in this forest or any other.

When I got back to the pickup, I peeled off my drenched clothes then sat listening to the rhythmic pounding of the torrent as I wrote down my thoughts. This would be my last journal entry from the National Forest and it took me back to my very first one, written in my tent by the light of an oil lantern, with Hunter snoring softly at the foot of my sleeping bag.

The time between those two entries had taught me more than I could have envisioned about this National Forest. It had changed my perspective on the Allegheny and, in some ways, my perspective on life. I better understood the history and policies that shape the face of the Forest and appreciated more than ever the passion that people who live, work, and hunt here feel for this rugged patch of ground.

Above all, it had been a great adventure. That's what I'll remember most about my season on the Allegheny.

ABOUT THE AUTHOR

Rob Hilliard has written on sports, history, and the outdoors for nearly two decades. Formerly a contributing editor with *Ohio Valley Outdoors* magazine, where he created the popular column, "In the Public Domain," Rob has also written numerous feature articles for magazines such as *Upland Almanac*, *Pennsylvania Wildlife*, *Pittsburgh History Magazine*, *ESPN Outdoors*, *Ohio Game and Fish*, and *Pennsylvania Game and Fish*. He was also a contributing author for the 2000 book *Rivers of Destiny*.

END NOTES

[1] "The History and Status of the Hemlock-Hardwood Forests of the Allegheny Plateau," Gordon G. Whitney, Journal of Ecology, Vol. 78, 1990.
[2] Ibid.
[3] Ibid.
[4] "Pennsylvania's Allegheny Hardwood Forests," David A. Marquis, Pennsylvania Forests, Vol. 63, No. 430, December 1973..
[5] Extinct Pennsylvania Animals, The Wolf Days, Henry W. Shoemaker, 1917.
[6] The Pennsylvania Game Commission 1895-1995 - 100 Years of Wildlife Conservation, Joe Kosack, Pennsylvania Game Commission, 1995.
[7] "Report on Deer Hunting Conditions in Allegheny National Forest for 1939," author unknown, Pennsylvania Game Commission, 1940.
[8] Elk County: A Journey through Time, Volume One – The Central Clarion Corridor, John Imhof, Clarion River Publishing, St. Marys, Pennsylvania, 2003.
[9] Ibid.
[10] Ibid.
[11] Ibid.
[12] "The Thousandth Acre," Reginald Forbes, American Forests, 1933.
[13] Ibid.
[14] Energy and Public Lands Report, The Wilderness Society, June 2000.
[15] "Tionesta Research Natural Area Oil, Gas, Mineral Rights Acquired," Conserve, Western Pennsylvania Conservancy, Vol. XXXI, No. Two, April 1988.
[16] Ibid.
[17] The Washington Times, Audrey Hudson, "ELF Admits to Arson," September 10, 2002, http://www.washingtontimes.com/national/20020910-1341902.htm
[18] "Activists Take over Allegheny National Forest Supervisor's Office," James Hansen, Earth First! press release, May 20, 1998.
[19] "Earth First! Financials," Center for Consumer Freedom, 2005, http://www.activistcash.com/organiztion_financials.cfm/oid/271.
[20] "One Terrible Week, Three Fearsome Fires," Wildland Firefighter, Vol. 2, No. 9, January 1999, Mike Schultz, pp.30-35.
[21] Ibid.
[22] Ibid.

[23] Sierra Club Statement on National Forest Protection and Restoration Act, Tue, 20 May 2003, Sierra Club Press Releases, Contact: Annie Strickler, http://lists.sierraclub.org/SCRIPTS/WA.EXE?A2=ind0305&L=cescnews-releases&D=1&T=0&H=1&O=D&F=&S=&P=1214
[24] "Activists Take Over Allegheny National Forest Supervisor's Office," 5/20/98, EarthFirst! News release, http://forests.org/archive/america/actoccal.htm
[25] "Forestry Expert Defends Management of Allegheny National Forest," Penn State Outdoor News Service press release, June 21, 2005.
[26] "Judge Gives OK to Allegheny National Forest Logging," Pittsburgh Post-Gazette, March 31, 2004, Associated Press.
[27] "Habitat Improvements Benefit Turkeys," Paul Frederick, Allegheny Online Magazine, http://www.allegheny-online.com/turkeyhabitat.html
[28] "Roosevelt's Tree Army," www.cccalumni.org/history1.html, June 18, 2005.
[29] Ibid.
[30] "The Admiration of the Entire Country," Excerpts from a message from the President of the United States to members of the CCC read over NBC network at 7:30 PM, Friday April 17, 1936, http://members.aol.com/famjustin/cccfdr1.html.
[31] "Roosevelt's Tree Army," www.cccalumni.org/history1.html, June 18, 2005.
[32] "Official Annual – 1936," Civilian Conservation Corps, District No.2, Third Corps Area, USA, p. 29.
[33] Ibid.
[34] Ibid.
[35] Schultz, 1999.
[36] "ATV Enthusiasts: Under Fire?," www.paatving.com/huntandfish/bmillsstory.asp, Brian Mills, June 2, 2005.
[37] "Stop Major 50-Mile ATV Trail Expansion Proposed for Allegheny National Forest!" http://www.alleghenydefense.org/alleghenywild/comments/willowcreekatv.htm
[38] "Report on Deer Hunting Conditions in Allegheny National Forest for 1939," Author Unknown, December 3, 1940.
[39] Ibid.
[40] "The Pennsylvania Deer Story 1958," Glen L. Bowers, Pennsylvania Game Commission, 1958.
[41] "The Deer Wars," Bob Marshall, Field and Stream, 110th Year, No. 3, July 2005, pp. 34-35.

[42] "Silviculture in Cooperation with Hunters: The Kinzua Quality Deer Cooperative," Scott Reitz, et al., USDA Forest Service Proceedings RMRS-P-34, 2004.
[43] "Tionesta Native had Hand in 1964 Preservation Act," by Ben Moyer, Pittsburgh Post-Gazette, September 5, 2004.
[44] "How Much Can We afford to Lose?" Howard Zahniser, Sierra Club Bulletin, April 1951.
[45] "Preserving Wilderness and Wildness as Enlarging the Boundaries of the Community," Ed Zahniser, http://www.wilderness.net/index.cfm?fuse=feature0504
[46] "Tionesta Native had Hand in 1964 Preservation Act," by Ben Moyer, Pittsburgh Post-Gazette, September 5, 2004.
[47] The soldier Dan referred to was Staff Sgt. Darren D. VanKomen, 33, of Bluefield, West Virginia, 2nd Squadron, 14th Cavalry Regiment, 1st Brigade, 25th Infantry Division.
[48] "Theodore Roosevelt - Hunter, Conservationist, President - Remains an Inspiration," Ken Barrett, Theodore Roosevelt Conservation Partnership, undated.
[49] "Gifford Pinchot (1865-1946): First Chief of the Forest Service, 1905-1910," Forest History Society, http://www.lib.duke.edu/forest//Research/usfscoll/people/Pinchot/Pinchot.html, November 2004
[50] Ibid.
[51] "Roosevelt the Hunter: Still America's Conservation Hero," National Shooting Sports Foundation, http://www.nssf.org/conservation/hero.cfm, undated.
[52] Ibid.
[53] Forest History Society, http://www.lib.duke.edu/forest//Research/usfscoll/policy/Wildlife/Index.html, November 2004.
[54] "Notes on the Settlement and Indian Wars," Joseph Doddridge, published by John S. Ritenour and William T. Lindsey, Pittsburgh, PA 1912.
[55] "Spiritual Laws," Ralph Waldo Emerson.
[56] "The Maine Woods," Henry David Thoreau, 1864, "The Writings of Henry David Thoreau," vol. 3, p. 242, Houghton Mifflin (1906).
[57] "Winter Fruits," Henry David Thoreau, Wild Fruits, Thoreau Institute at Walden Woods, http://www.walden.org/Institute/thoreau/writings/fruits/Fruits_06.htm, circa 1862.
[58] "The Puritan Origins of the American Wilderness Movement," J. Baird Callicott, "Wilderness and American Identity" Essays, National

Humanities Center, http://www.nhc.rtp.nc.us:8080/tserve/nattrans/ntwilderness/essays/puritanb.htm, undated.
[59] "The Kinzua Dam: Progress or Perfidy," George H. Moeller, USDA Forest Service, NCFES, St. Paul, MN, Spring, 1971.
[60] "Roots of Seneca anger," Michael Beebe, The Buffalo News, July 6, 2003.
[61] "The Kinzua Dam: Progress or Perfidy," George H. Moeller, USDA Forest Service, NCFES, St. Paul, MN, Spring, 1971.
[62] "Roots of Seneca anger," Michael Beebe, The Buffalo News, July 6, 2003.
[63] Ibid.
[64] "The American Sportsman: Take a Closer Look," Congressional Sportsmen's Foundation and National Shooting Sports Foundation, Inc., November 2004.
[65] "Green Utopia – Rural Ruination," Douglas E. Carlson, The Environmental Conservation Organization Inc., http://www.eco.freedom.org/articles/dougcarlson-904.html, 2004.

Made in the USA
Lexington, KY
18 November 2012